The E
of
Jesus

Calling a Generation into
Radical Devotion

A Compilation of Dreams, Visions,
and Prophetic Encounters

JOMA OKWUMABUA SHORT

TRILOGY
A WHOLLY OWNED SUBSIDIARY OF TBN
PROFESSIONAL PUBLISHING MEETS POWERFUL PROMOTION

The Beauty of Jesus: Calling a Generation into Radical Devotion

Trilogy Christian Publishers
A Wholly Owned Subsidiary of Trinity Broadcasting Network
2442 Michelle Drive, Tustin, CA 92780

10 9 8 7 6 5 4 3 2 1
Library of Congress Cataloging-in-Publication Data is available.

ISBN: 979-8-88738-958-5
E-ISBN: 979-8-88738-959-2

ENDORSEMENTS

"This book is a clear and provoking invitation to run into the heart of the Father by experiencing the Person of Jesus. Joma's book outlines years of insight, testimonies, and encounters that will encourage you to walk in the fullness of your design. She simply combines truth, humility, and the Spirit's power. This generation will benefit much from the principles communicated in this book. I encourage anyone to read this book. It will touch your heart in new ways with the beauty of Jesus."

— Stuart Greaves
Executive Director at the International House of
Prayer Missions Base in Kansas City, Missouri
www.ihopkc.org

"One of the highest honors and responsibilities we have is to impact the emerging generation, and to ensure our ceiling, and the ceilings of generations before us becomes their floor. This book is indeed such a ceiling, and my prayer is that many will be inspired to run higher and faster toward the beauty of Jesus as they stand on that ceiling."

— Daphne Kirk
Founder of Generation 2 Generation
https://g2gmandate.org/

"In *The Beauty of Jesus*, Joma Short inspires readers with her personal testimonies of pursuing a relationship with Jesus and experiencing powerful encounters with God. Her story reveals that we are never too young to seek the Lord. Despite its focus on the next generation, this book encourages and challenges all generations to set aside distractions and surrender all as we faithfully live for God and seek the peace and power of His presence."

— Dr. Jolene Erlacher
Next Gen Author and Speaker
www.leadingtomorrow.org

"*The Beauty of Jesus* contains a message for the body of Christ today. The message is that Jesus is worthy of pursuing with everything we have. The time is short. Believers must seek Jesus with passion to prepare themselves and others for His return. Joma shares her beautiful experiences of encountering the love of Jesus as a way of encouraging others. Reading this book will ignite a fresh hunger in your heart to know Jesus and His love for all people. To God be the glory!"

— Dr. Michael Peters
Director of the IHOPE House of Prayer
The Nations TV, Waterloo, Iowa
www.ihopehouseofprayer.com
www.thenationstv.com

"There are some people who answer the invitation to draw closer into a friendship relationship with the Father. Those who answer the invitation are shown some of the deep things that are on the Father's heart and have a unique relationship with Him. Joma is one of those people. I hope you read between the lines of revelation that are shared in this book and that it leads you to draw close to Him as well."

— Stephen Harmon
Senior Pastor at Kingdom Life Community Church,
Morrison, Illinois
www.kingdomlife.global

"Not surprised; I've had the privilege of looking into the eyes of many young men and women, and in them, I've seen dreams and aspirations. I have also had the honor of being inspired by them, and the humbling thought that I could be an inspiration to them. And though I saw many dreams die for lack of cultivation, something in the eyes of Joma, something of determination and passion. Something of perseverance and genuine love for her Savior and Lord Jesus brings me to say, "I'm not surprised that she has chosen to be the means by which God speaks to this generation. I believe you will be moved, stirred, and encouraged through the insights and experiences of this godly servant of the Lord."

— Pastor Dan Hernandez
Senior Pastor of Water of Life Ministries,
Rockford, Illinois

"I first met Joma as a student in my class at North Central University. During that time, it became evident that she is a leader and a person attuned to the Spirit of God. We developed a bond that has lasted through the years. My wife and I have supported Joma's ministry, followed her career, and personally been blessed by her prophetic gifting. Joma is a worshiper who seeks the heart of God. I pray that, like us, you will be blessed by her ministry as you read her life's stories."

— Philip Mayo, Ph.D.
President and International Teacher
Ville Lumière, Paris Ministries, Inc.
villeluierefr.com

"Joma Short has been a part of our lives for over twenty years. We know her to be a strong and unapologetic advocate for the Kingdom of God. When we received the communication from her about the book she has written, *The Beauty of Jesus*, we were excited because we know her and, moreover, we know her motivation. Jomas's motivation is the same as it has been since the day we met: for the next generation.

"This, of course, is rooted in Malachi 4:6, where it gives a promise from the Lord to 'turn the heart of the fathers to the children, and the heart of the children to their fathers' (KJV). We believe parenting ministry is essential for the growth of believers and presents a deeper, more enduring intergenerational bond. When the disciples asked Jesus to teach them how to pray, Jesus revealed God as a parent—a Father.

"The apostle Paul reminds us that spiritual parents are rare, indeed. First Corinthians 4:15 says: *For though you might have ten thousand instructors in Christ, yet you do not have many fa-*

thers.' We are excited for the testimony of this book and pray that it turns the hearts of our generations to God, and to one another. It is without reservation that Joma receives our highest recommendation."

— Pastor John and Lynn Magee
Senior Pastors at Light The Way Church,
Cottage Grove, Minnesota
www.lightthewaychurch.com

DEDICATION

I dedicate this book to the upcoming generation of singers, musicians, songwriters, artisans, scribes, playwrights, Nazirites, prophets, apostles, teachers, preachers, evangelists, and lovers of Jesus. Run your race! Jesus is gloriously beautiful, and He is more than enough to satisfy every desire of your creative and artistic heart.

> *Give unto the LORD, O you mighty ones,*
> *Give unto the LORD glory and strength.*
> *Give unto the LORD the glory due to His name;*
> *Worship the LORD in the beauty of holiness.*

> —Psalm 29:1–2

CONTENTS

CHAPTER 1
The First Encounter

And the Angel of the LORD said to him, "Why do you ask My name, seeing it is wonderful?"

— Judges 13:18

As a young person, I always felt like I was unusual. I knew I was made for more than what I had become. While I knew society, culture, and life had created a path for me to journey upon, I also knew that those paths seemed superficial, fake, and even undesirable. My heart wanted to know about the deeper things of life. I needed to know whether there was more to life than just living it. Getting an education and gaining a career, a marriage, a house with a white picket fence and 2.5 kids, and a dog, were, for some reason, not too appealing to me.

A life in the fast lane did not appeal to me, either. Drugs, alcohol, sex, and all the things the culture glorified as "stardom and popularity" seemed desperately hollow and fleeting in substance. Why would I share my body with someone who did not value me as a person? Why would I spend time and energy to get out of my right mind? Why would I chase money, cars, and possessions? Glamour seemed to be a mere Band-Aid to the searching soul. In time, I watched the rich, famous, and talented all commit suicide. My observation was true. Money, riches, awards, and accolades do not satisfy the deepest desire of the human heart. Only our Creator can do such a thing. I had to know more. I had to discover the truth.

That realization settled my inner turmoil. I had to know. *Jesus, are You real? If You are real, then are You the only way? If You are the only way, then why?* My heart cry became, "Jesus, if You are really the True and Living God, then reveal Yourself to me." I had to know whether He was real. I was not going to spend my life serving a fictitious God if He was not the True and Living Way. I did not want to waste my time and words telling people about a God who was not the True and Almighty God.

THE SEPARATION

In response to my inward desire for more, I decided to go on a journey myself and discover if Jesus was really the Truth. I committed myself to three months of separation. As a thirteen-year-old, I chose to seek the Lord for three months in an intentional and focused way. Here are my commitments for that time:

1. For three months, I committed to spend every waking moment that I was not in school or playing sports actively seeking the Presence of the Lord. I spent time either in my bedroom or in a church sanctuary, praying, worshiping, and just waiting on God. I was given access to two

sanctuaries in town. My pastor at the church I attended on Sundays gave me a key to come in any time, day or night, to spend time in worship and prayer. He saw my desire to seek the Lord, and to this day I thank him for providing space for me to linger. The church where I began to attend youth group also opened their sanctuary for prayer for any of us youth who wanted to come in and pray. So many days after school and even into the night, I buried my face in the walls of that sanctuary, as well.

2. I committed to read the Bible as my only form of literature. I walked away from all television, movies, and other forms of entertainment. I purchased my first Bible concordance and Bible dictionary and set my face to see if the Bible was as special as some said it was.

3. I abstained from friends, relationships, the appeal of the opposite sex, and anything else that could take my attention and focus as a teenager away from the Lord.

4. I committed to attend every church service on Wednesday and Sunday, take notes, and listen intently to what the pastor taught.

During those three months, I felt the increase of the Presence of the Lord in my life in every way. As I spent time in prayer, I wept often under the tangible weight of His Presence. It seemed at times that the entire atmosphere of my bedroom began to shift into another realm. I had never experienced such a Presence before. The air became thick, and it moved around like an invisible wave of electrifying power. Then, in time, the Presence began to speak. But He spoke not as a loud voice from without; rather, He spoke from a clarity and a power that came from within. I thought, *Who is this that speaks from within? Who is this who speaks with such power, yet is so loud from within?*

At times I'd be weeping so loudly and uncontrollably that my mom would come into my bedroom to ask if I was okay. But as she opened my bedroom door, she would see me sitting in the dark with a candle lit as tissues lay all about the floor. I just waved my arm to her, saying, "Yes, I am fine. God is just speaking to me." So, she would close the door and walk away. I think I was a bit much for her. I am not sure if she understood what was happening, but she gave me space to continue in my secret pursuit.

My candle stood to me as a visual representation of my prayer. I knew that as I looked at the candle and the wax began to melt and transform, something was also changing inside of me. I fought the lies in my head telling me that I was wasting my time, energy, and words speaking to an invisible entity way off in the distance. I knew His Presence was melting my heart, much like the fire of the candle melted the wax all around the inflamed wick.

As I began to read the Word, the first two books of the Bible that stood out to me to read from start to finish were the book of Acts and the book of the Revelation of Jesus Christ. *Why not start at the end?* I figured. Little did I know, these two books contained the answers to the deepest desires of my thirteen-year-old heart.

I quickly discovered that the Word of God, the Bible, was true. It was different from any book I had ever read. It was the first Book that seemed to read me, instead of the other way around. This Book was alive, and every time I opened its pages, I was pulled into another realm.

There was a time when my mom fell ill, and my siblings called the ambulance to rush her to the hospital. In the middle of the panic, I remembered something I had read in the Bible. The words of the Bible were clear in saying that the Spirit of Jesus heals. If I would pray in His name and with His authority, then I would see the same results. So, as I waited for the ambulance to come and my mom faded into unconsciousness, I decided to take matters into my own hands. My hands began to burn like flames of fire, and then I put my hands on her forehead and commanded all sickness to leave her body under the authority and the power of the blood of Jesus. I said, "Be healed in Jesus' name!"

Within seconds, she came to herself. I asked her what happened, and she said she was starting to feel better—and she could even sit up. She told us not to call the ambulance, but she didn't realize that we had already done just that. She told us that she heard a loud popping sound, and then all the pressure left her head and body. She said the pressure that left from the top of her head felt immense and that she was feeling much better now. I knew then that every word of the Bible was true. I knew in that moment that the Bible was real, that it was powerful and to be taken seriously.

As the three months went on, I continued to feel the power and the tangible Presence of the Lord, but I was wanting more. As the days slipped by, I found myself becoming forlorn and a little depressed. I knew God was real. I knew His Word was true. But I was hoping He would be "better" than what I had experienced. I wanted more from Him. I did not want to give myself to a God who was far off, but I wanted to know the God of Wonders. I needed to know that He was worth me giving all of myself to.

I found myself finishing the last of days of my commitment out of obligation, but my heart grew weary. I was hoping that Jesus would be more exhilarating. I thought He would be more satisfying. In my heart, I was contemplating just living life the way I wanted. I once heard one of my favorite rappers at the time say, "Life is a b**** and then you die… still trying to get a piece of that apple pie." I was beginning to think maybe he was right. Maybe the American dream and self-pleasure were the best this world had to offer.

THE ENCOUNTER

Then finally, it came—the last Sunday of my vow. During the length of my time of consecration, I had arranged rides for someone to pick me up or drop me off for church services because my family did not attend church. This particular Sunday, I did not feel like going to church, but because I had said I would go, I woke up and got dressed. Little did I know that in a few hours, my life was going to change forever.

The church service began, and after the singing was done, the pastor began to speak about salvation and how Jesus came to save. I was bored. Very bored. I had heard this message before what seemed like a thousand times already. I wanted to hear something new, something I had never heard before, something I could not attain on my own. The harsh reality was that I'd had more exciting and powerful times with the Lord when I was alone in my bedroom than I did when I was in church.

So, I just tuned out and did not listen to another word the pastor was speaking. My mind began to wander on to sports and food. I knew the Chicago Bears, my favorite football team, was playing in the afternoon, and being the true Bears fans that we were, my family would serve lots of good food and invite cousins, aunts, uncles, and any other stragglers over to our house to watch the games. I figured I would turn my sights back to the temporal pleasures that sports, gatherings, and food provided.

I purposefully sat on the very last row of the church directly next to the exit sign. I figured as soon as he dismissed everyone, I would be free to go back to life as usual. But to my surprise, Holy Spirit began to grab my attention. My mind suddenly went from pondering football and food to being acutely alert. I began to look around the room, and my vision became cloudy. It was like smoke and clouds began to fill the room. I kept blinking my eyes, thinking maybe my eyes were just blurry, but then I began to feel dizzy as well. As these things were happening, the pastor stopped speaking, then interrupted his message to say the Lord wanted him to speak to someone there today in a special way. He said, "I feel there is someone here today who is sick and tired of being sick and tired. And you need to *surrender* your life to Jesus."

That was it. He was speaking directly to me, and I knew it. I felt like the pastor had put all my business and heart on display in front of everyone. How dare he? But how did he know? And where did those words come from? I knew he was speaking directly to me. His words were like an arrow of revelation going straight through my heart. I was exposed and laid bare before Him.

I then realized his words were true. I had never heard the message of surrender before. All I ever heard was, "Give your heart to Jesus." And I had done that before, but the act of giving Him my heart had never been enough to satisfy my soul. I still didn't have peace and fulfillment. But in this message of surrender, I knew my vow was nothing but a vapor. I thought my three months of separation and seeking God was a major undertaking. I had asked God all types of questions. I had even challenged His goodness as a deity. But in that moment, I realized—for the first time—that Jesus gave *everything* for me. Jesus literally poured out His entire life for me. He gave all for me, and it was only fitting for me to do the same. Jesus is a good leader—yes, the perfect leader. He never asks or requires His people to give or do anything that He Himself has not already done or given.

I knew I needed to surrender to Him. It was as if Holy Spirit caused my entire life to flash before my eyes—all my goals, aspirations, career paths, athletic endeavors, the desire for wealth, and accomplishments. I knew I needed to lay it all down. I knew I needed to erase the whiteboard of my life and let Jesus fill it with whatever He desired. I needed to surrender all, not just give Him my heart. I needed to make Him my Lord and my Leader. I needed to give Him everything—everything I currently was and everything I would eventually become.

In my thirteen-year-old heart, the pause felt like an eternity, but I decided within myself to respond. I counted the cost.

I counted the loss. I relinquished control of my own destiny, and I chose to give Jesus the pen in the storybook of my life. To this day, I am not certain what happened next. I do not remember walking down to the front of the church. But somehow, I found myself standing there in front of everyone. I had run to the altar and fallen on my knees. I was going to open up my mouth and say, "Jesus, I give You my life. I surrender it all to You." But just as I opened my mouth, other languages began to flow out of my mouth. A violent, rushing power from above came into my body and up out of my mouth.

I began to shake, and then I realized I could not stop speaking in this new Holy Spirit–given language. Tears flowed down my face, and I couldn't see enough to grab a tissue to wipe my now-flowing nose. All I could do was tremble underneath the power of the Holy Spirit. I knew not to be afraid of what was happening because I remembered what I had read in the book of Acts. In my room a few weeks prior, I had read what happened when tongues of fire came and filled the Upper Room where the disciples had gathered, waiting for the promised Gift. I had asked for it for myself while alone in my room weeks ago, and nothing seemed to happen—but now, in His sovereignty, He had answered my prayer.

Before I knew what was happening, the sanctuary of the church began to feel small. I opened my eyes and saw my spirit leaving my body. I actually looked down at myself and was perplexed. I was completely myself, yet when I looked, my body was kneeling directly beneath me. I heard all the voices of the people in the church, and I heard some of them praying over me. But I lost all feeling in my body, and my spirit began to go up into the heavens. I was not sure what was happening, but

I knew it was holy. I felt His peace. Unknown tongues were still coming out of my mouth in my physical body, but that was the last I remembered of my physical self. My body still was kneeling facedown on the floor, still wearing my white blouse and long black skirt. Yet up I went.

I went higher and higher, and everything became black. Then the black began to turn into a deep blue color. I then began to soar higher, even above the stars and galaxies. I went right through them. Then everything became loud—very loud. The sounds were so intense that I wanted to cover my ears, but there was no escaping it.

As I continued to look up, there was a Rushing River that whipped and spun all across the heavens. The River was alive, and it rushed here and there. The River was alive, and it acted like a Person. The River had personality, and it flowed wherever it desired. There were many twists and turns, different patterns and ways the River flowed. After I'd spent some time watching it, the River came directly at me. It somehow came into my body. The River came into the top of my head and filled my entire being. Then it came up out of me and flowed mightily out of my mouth. I knew in that moment that the Holy Spirit was rewiring me and making me a mouthpiece and an instrument of His using. This water was the Living Water. This water was the Spirit of Living Water. As the water filled me and my entire being, it began to flow out of my mouth with even greater force.

The River flowed through me for some time, and then I realized I was in a stationary location. I looked around and found I was standing in the middle of what appeared to be a rushing river. It looked like a large moat in the way that it flowed. This body of water was different from the first Living Water I had encountered. The appearance of the water was like dazzling crystal. The river looked like pieces of glass, with a beautiful spectrum of blues, silvers, and white inside of it. I stood in the middle of this glass-like sea and thought I might die or be cut into pieces by the glass. The entire scene was charged with power. I did not see any way of escaping the glassy sea. I felt like someone had stuck me there in the middle of it. Then *whoa*—a wave came and crashed over me!

When the crystal sea crashed over me, the force of a thousand hammers came and crushed my spirit in that sea. The sea was alive. And Someone had intentionally placed me there, sticking me in the middle of it.

After that first wave crashed over me, I realized I was not hurt. Not one cut, not one scrape. I was still fully intact. But I had become lighter. Then *whoa!* Another wave came. This one crashed over me with even more force. Again, I felt lighter. I was being delivered from oppression, depressions, generational curses possibly in my bloodline, and other things of which I was not even aware. Again, wave after wave crashed over me, and I became lighter and lighter. I felt free—freer than I knew I could ever experience. After what seemed to be about ten minutes in the natural, the waves no longer crashed over me. I felt so light at that point I thought I was going to float away into a higher region of the space.

Then I looked over past the sea of crystal and saw a bright light. I had never seen a light this bright before. The light shined the purest white—yes, beyond white in color. The crisp purity of this light was beyond the whitest white I'd ever seen. The spectrum of the color was piercing and almost blinding.

The light was piercing, yet alluring, so alluring that I could not look away, though I had to squint my eyes just to keep looking.

The light shone brighter and brighter. The luminescence surrounding it gained more definition. The light was moving. The light was coming toward me. After some time, I realized the light was actually a Person—and that Person was coming right toward me. That Person was Jesus Himself.

His glory was beyond anything I can put into words, but even in the midst of the sea of glass, my spirit began to shake. I somehow knew my body back on earth was shaking as well. I thought I was going to die. My thoughts were, *Wow. I got saved just to die!* Then Jesus looked right at me and smirked affectionately.

The smirk transformed into a smile that communicated a thousand words. He knew me. He knew me inside and out. He had heard every question, every challenge of His goodness, His perfection, His deity, His authority, and Him being the only way. The closer He came to me, the more I began to feel I was going slip away into oblivion. My spirit could not withstand that type of glory. At one point, in my mind, I had to tell my spirit to breathe. Just keep breathing. Every breath was an effort. My tongue clung to the roof of my mouth.

I finally tried to put up my arm and beg Him not to come any closer. I knew it. I knew He was restraining His glory just so my un-resurrected body and spirit could withstand His holy Presence. And before He said anything, I knew He was everything He said He was. I knew in that moment that He was the First and the Last. I knew He was the everlasting God. He was and is and will forever be the most beautiful Man I've ever met.

I knew I could spend every hour of every day just searching Him out, and I knew I would just be getting to the edges of Him. His goodness and His beauty are far beyond our comprehension. In that moment, I found my One Thing. He became the very endeavor of life itself. Life for me, both now and forever, will consist of my pursuit of this Man.

After we had communicated for some time, the encounter shifted. I went into a visionary state. Jesus ascended and became the Sun in the sky. I somehow thought, *The Sun/Son of Righteousness will rise with healing in His wings*. I longed for Him to stay, but I knew the encounter was out of my control.

I saw myself on a stage. There was a large outdoor platform and stage in the middle of what seemed to be a desert. I stood on the stage with a microphone in my hand. Behind me, there were speakers and musical instruments. On the stage, there was a person standing next to me, and down on the other end of the stage, I saw a few more standing. The guy standing next to me also had a microphone in his hand, and he was full of the presence of the Lord—to the extent that it appeared as though he'd leap off of the stage straight in the air.

I had an air and a confidence about me that I never had seen or experienced before that time. There was a power and authority to my words that caused me, even looking at this vision, to tremble. I only said one thing: "Worship the Lord in Spirit and in truth!" When I made this statement in the vision, it was as though a sonic boom left my mouth and went out into the atmosphere. I had never heard such words before, but from what I saw, it caused me to think, *Wow. Yes, that sounds so good! I believe it. I agree. What a powerful and clear thought! Worship the Lord in Spirit and in truth.*

I began to wonder, To whom was I talking in the vision? And why was there a stage set up in the middle of the wilderness? Then, as I mentally asked myself the question, the intensity of the Sun/Son backed off a bit, to the point that I could see all around from different angles. My view changed into a panoramic perspective. I saw, from the base of the stage and out to the horizon, a sea of young people. There seemed to be millions of them. They all fell facedown, prostrate, before the Lord of Hosts. A few were on their knees, but most were on their faces. A weighty fear of the Lord rested upon the entire crowd, and the Holy Spirit focused in on a few of their faces. I knew they were ones whom Jesus Himself was assigning me to influence. I somehow knew I would cross paths with these people in life, and I was to pour into them all the goodness the Lord had shown to me.

I had never seen anything like this before—such awe, sobriety, power, authority, and wonder. And the Presence rested upon the entire assembly. I thought to myself, as my spirit was gazing upon myself in the vision, *I believe that declaration!* I began to believe those words. I could see myself doing that. It wasn't until years later that I realized those words were from Scripture, and that vision was my life calling flashing before my spiritual eyes. I had been created to worship Jesus and to call forth this generation to worship Him in Spirit and in truth.

After seeing the crowds going all the way to the horizon, I began to sink back into my body. I was not going back according to my own will, but I began to sink and the colors began to lose their brightness. I fell through the clouds and the vast dark expanse. Then, before I knew what was happening, I fell right back into my body. The church was silent and empty.

Where had everyone gone? How long had I been out of my body?

I felt like a new person. I barely even recognized my own body. It was almost as if I had to remember how to use it properly. I did not remember lying down on my back—the last I remember, I had been kneeling—but I began to peel myself off the floor. Too dizzy to stand, I fell over onto the floor again. I think the noise and commotion of that caused my pastor to return to the sanctuary and attend to me. My pastor and his wife were the only two people left in the building, and she was in the downstairs portion of the church. My pastor came in from the foyer and helped me to stand and walk. After a few minutes of silence, he said, with his Mexican-American accent, "The Lord really touched you, didn't He?"

I opened my mouth to try to respond, but I could barely make eye contact with him, and when I opened my mouth to speak, more tongues came flying out. *Oh no!* I thought: *I am going up again.* My spirit began to lift out of my body again, my knees buckled, and my body gave way and fell to the ground. "Whoa… whoa!" my pastor yelled as his wife came up from the basement area.

I could not speak anything but tongues for hours. I had no words or control over my mouth if I opened it. So, I finally stopped trying to talk. My pastor and his wife helped me get into my mother's car. Apparently, she had been waiting for me ever since the service was over. No one from my family attended church regularly at that time, so I had to arrange rides. To this day, I do not remember how long I was "gone" in the natural. I just remember my pastors laying me down in the back seat of my mom's car, while her suspicious and slightly frightened eyes looked at me through the rearview mirror. To make it worse, I couldn't even talk to try to tell her what happened.

For years, I did not tell a soul everything that transpired that day. The encounter was far too sacred, and I needed to make sense of everything in my own heart. The few times I began to share an abbreviated version of the encounter, I was met with fear, cynicism, doubt, or bewilderment, so I kept it to myself. I simply pondered these things in my heart, and in secret, I began to follow Jesus with all of my heart, mind, soul, and strength.

I began to listen to Him and treat Him as the Person of value that He was. He became the object of my affection, the One to whom I was wholly devoted.

Takeaway

Jesus is gloriously beautiful, and He is worth a life that is fully given to Him. I encourage you to take a time of separation for yourself. My separation was three months long, but whatever the Holy Spirit leads you to do as a time frame, do it. Separate yourself from the world and anything that pulls at your attention. When I was younger, I learned it took ninety days to create a new habit, so that is why I chose ninety days for my time of separation. But I urge you to set aside an amount of time that feels like a sacrifice to you.

Separate yourself from media, entertainment, literature, people, and any other sources of potential distraction. Then set your gaze solely upon Jesus. During the duration of your consecration, spend every waking moment possible in His Presence.

Read and meditate on Scriptures in the Bible. Sit in prayer and conversation with Jesus, Abba Father, and Holy Spirit. Let them talk to you and respond appropriately. Ask Him what He thinks about you and why He created you. Jesus is a Person. Spend time with Him just like you would spend with a friend or any other person whom you desire to get to know more intimately.

He does not share the deep things of His heart with everyone. He reserves the secrets of His heart for His close friends.

The choice is yours. Will you be a follower? Or will you be a friend?

Prayer of Impartation

Now hold out your hands in front of yourself, as if you are receiving a gift. I bless you with these words in prayer. I pray that what rests upon me and in me transfers unto you with a Spirit of burning and fire.

> *Father of Glory, I raise my hands and I bless this generation that is coming forward. I ask that Your loving-kindness and tender mercy chase them down. I ask that those who truly hunger and thirst after You will find You and be satisfied. Lord, come and satisfy the deepest desires of their searching hearts. I ask that they come fully out of darkness and step into Your Light. Let each one realize his or her full potential in You, and may they love You with all their hearts, souls, minds, and strength. Lord, I pray for an opening up of the revelatory realm. What rests on me, may it come and rest upon them. I declare an opening of spiritual*

eyes, ears, and hearts. I bless their human spirits with peace, light, and shekinah glory. The very entry of Your Word brings light, so I declare a breaking in of light. Light of Jesus, come and fill every empty place in them Lord, I pray they will engage and interact with You using all their natural and spiritual senses. I pray for an opening up of throne-room encounters and Holy Spirit travel before the throne of our heavenly Father. Father of our spirits, I bless the reader and commit their ways to You, with the mighty authority that Jesus gave. Amen.

CHAPTER 2

Lovesickness

"I charge you, O daughters of Jerusalem, if you find my beloved, that you tell him I am lovesick!"

— Song of Solomon 5:8

THE EYES OF THE LORD

In the previous chapter, you learned of my encounter with Jesus that took place when I was thirteen years old. That occurred during the summer of 1997. Years went by, and my love and affection for Jesus grew. Though I attended a school of accelerated learning for the academically gifted, and I could have attended any Ivy League school I desired, I chose to give my life to the Bible, the study of the Word, and a life of ministry and missions. Against the will of my teachers, parents, and coaches, I attended a Bible school to attain a ministry degree.

After a few years of college, I found my schedule becoming busy and full of activities, all of which left an ache in my heart for Jesus, and a desire to spend time with Him. I was a full-time student with a heavier course load than most because I was squeezing two majors into one degree. I was actively involved with leadership in campus ministry and ministry in the city of Minneapolis. And I was a student-athlete, playing both volleyball and softball. My schedule left me busy most days and nights, but my heart longed for more of the Lord.

One day after volleyball practice and a late dinner, I went and lay on my bed. I knew I had to work on a paper that was due soon, and I also had a meeting to attend later in the evening. But my heart ached. I needed more of Jesus. I did not want to do another activity. I missed alone time with Him. So, I lay on my lofted bunk bed in my dorm room and raised my hands to the ceiling. "Jesus. I miss You. I need You. I want You."

Within a few minutes, the space over my bed began to open, and I began to see clouds come into the room. It was as if a portal had opened right there above me in my dorm room. I saw thick clouds—and then I began to see a familiarly wonderful face. The clouds began to part, and I saw His forehead, then His brow, then finally His eyes. There it stopped. His eyes were on me. All He did was gaze at me. I don't remember Him even blinking. He just stared into my soul.

His eyes were like deep wells of truth and glory. Eternity dwelt within them. As I gazed into His eyes, it was clear there was no end to Him. His eyes were serious and full of authority as He gazed at me. His authority was mixed with a love and knowledge that I cannot express with words.

He finally turned and broke our stare—it was as if someone or something else had called for His attention. He briefly looked away, then He looked at me once again, as to give me a final glance, saying, *Bye for now*. From that moment, I began to move into a vision. I saw myself on a long road, walking on a long hard journey, one that would require me to pick up my own cross and follow Him. The Lord began to tell me that I would have a long, hard journey before me, but that He would be with me every step of the way. Though my journey would be arduous and long, I would endure to the end with great joy. Just keep looking to Him, He said. He would never leave me alone.

Then, just like that, He was gone. The vision was over. I could barely breathe. I want you to know: Jesus is so beautiful. His eyes alone are beyond comparison. Second Chronicles 16:9 says it well: "The eyes of the LORD run to and fro throughout the whole earth, to show Himself strong on behalf of those whose heart is loyal to Him." I counted it a privilege to have His eyes fall on me. Come what may, I will trust and follow Him until the end of my days!

Takeaway

Life gets busy at times. Sometimes busyness keeps us from those who are closest to us, including our beautiful King Jesus. My obligations as a young scholar-athlete and campus leader kept my schedule busy. At times, the best thing I did to get alone time with Jesus was to skip a meal or two and spend that time with Him in my personal prayer closet.

My second option was to spend time with Him late in the night when everyone else around me was asleep. My encouragement to you is to protect and guard your time with Jesus. Treat Him with the honor and respect you would give a significant other or anyone else whom you highly value in your life. Do not just give Him your leftover time but carve out segments of your day that are truly for only Him and you. True life consists of intimate moments that fuel our mundane, day-to-day tasks. Alone time with Jesus will give you the courage and passion you need to live out your other daily tasks in life.

Lift your hands and open your spirit to receive this prayer blessing.

Father, I bless this generation that is coming forward. I bless them with the gift of lovesickness, spiritual thirst, and spiritual hunger. Father, I pray they do not fill their hearts, thought lives, soul realms, and spirits with substances that do not truly satisfy.

I pray that those who truly desire and seek after You will find You. Lord, may they seek You with all their hearts. Jesus, Your words of prophecy were true when You said, "Surely, you will love the Lord your God with all of your heart, soul, mind, and strength" (see Deuteronomy 6:5; Matthew 22:37; Luke 10:27). Lord, let the ache within them grow to the point that they leave everything behind to follow You. Let Your loving-kindness and tender mercy chase them down. I release the Living Water from above to come and baptize them in your eternal goodness.

CLOTHED IN DARKNESS

I was still in my sophomore year of college. A familiar feeling came over me: I wanted more. But this time I went from a deep longing all the way to lovesickness. I was lovesick for the Lord. I had a long to-do list in my daily life, but only one thing sounded appealing to me: I wanted alone time with my Jesus. I didn't know how much time I would be able to steal away. But I would lock my dorm room door and lay on the floor. My heart ached. *Jesus! I need another touch from You.*

As I lay there on the floor one day, I saw a dark figure enter my room. I sat up and began to rebuke it: "Every foul and unclean spirit, I rebuke you in the name and authority of Jesus. I don't have any time for you right now. Get out of here. Only Jesus and His holy Angels are welcome here."

That was all. I lay back down. That day I had absolutely no grace for interference or evil spirits. As I lay back on the floor, a flash of light suddenly came around my feet. *What was that? I* thought. *Didn't I tell the darkness to flee?!* Then, before I had another thought, I slipped into the spirit realm. I was lying on the floor in the exact same position, but I was seeing into the spirit realm, and I was fully awake. (The best way I can explain the crossing over in that moment was when, in the movies *The Lord of the Rings*, Frodo the hobbit puts on his ring, he goes into another realm. Without that "ring of power," my spirit moved over into the spirit realm.)

As I lay there on the floor, a tall, hooded person approached me. As he came close, I saw that his clothes were not black, but a deep purple color. Why the hood and the veil? Who was this? Before I could speak, though, I felt a familiar Presence. A peace came over me. It was the Lord. He turned, looked at me, and spoke one word. Then He reached down to touch my chest. He placed His right hand upon me.

As He spoke, it was like the corridors of glory opened and waterfalls and rushing rivers poured out. His voice bounced off the dimensions and within and through every barrier known to creation. His voice tore the very cells of my body apart, and I began to scream. I screamed so loud that I ended the entire encounter. I screamed with such terror that I slipped back into the natural realm. There I lay on the floor—and apparently, I was screaming in the natural.

Overcome by what had just happened, I did not hear someone pounding on my door for several minutes. Some of my friends and neighbors had called campus security to bust down the door to see if I was okay. I finally called to them that I was fine. When they asked me what had happened, if someone was hurting me, I did not know how to respond. I told them I was fine… that I had just seen a mouse. I lied! *Lord Jesus, forgive me.* That was the best excuse I could come up with.

Jesus Himself had come to deliver a message to me, and I freaked out! Not to mention, I had rebuked Him at first, thinking His dark cloak was an evil presence. I can't believe I did that. I was so mad at myself. How can you scream your way out of a holy moment?! I only got the first word of what He wanted to say! And also, I had lied about there being a mouse.

Takeaway

The Lord Jesus desires time with us more than we desire time with Him. We, as humans, in this time of *His story* (aka history) are limited in many of our capacities. Jesus, however, is limitless and dwells outside of time; He is Lord of all. Whether it be dimensions, realms, principalities, thrones, or powers, Jesus is seated far above them all.

When we go into the secret place, yes, we must be intentional to make time with Him in our daily and weekly schedules. But as we go into our secret place, we must remember that Jesus may take us somewhere else. He may take us into another realm or dimension. He may take us up to heavenly places. We may be "gone" for what seems like hours or even days, but then we may come back into our bodies in the natural realm and only minutes have passed on our side of the veil.

Jesus is not boring, friends! He is the King of the entire universe. He sits enthroned over all realms, dimensions, timelines, and multiverses, on into eternity and beyond. He shares deep and unsearchable things with His friends. So again, I ask you, "Are you going to be a follower, or are you going to be His friend?"

Prayer of Impartation

Raise your hands, open your spirit, and receive this prayer of blessing.

> *Father, for those who are wanting more of You, I bless them with sonship. Lord, I ask that they will come forth in their identity as a son of God and that they would also come forth in their identity as the bride of*

Christ. I ask that their spiritual eyes will be opened to see what is the hope of their calling in You.

You are the One who created all things and made the worlds, and You continue to sustain and uphold them by the Word of Your power. Reveal to them that they have been given full access to Your kingdom. Help them understand that everything that belongs to You, Jesus, now belongs to them as well. As Arthur Burk has said, "Slaves obey, but sons create." I bless them not only with servitude, but with the identity of sonship.

I bless them in coming into the fullness of their design. May they walk in love and the authority and the power of Jesus Himself. I seal this prayer in every age, time, realm, and dimension by the power of your blood, Jesus.

GOING UP

After much reflection, I coached myself to relax. I told myself that during the next encounter I would maintain my composure and be calmer. I would not let my flesh win, but I would yield to the Holy Spirit as He led me. A few months later, I was lying on my couch in the same dorm room. I was supposed to be studying, but instead I was daydreaming about the Lord.

I was preparing to go on a mission trip within a few months, and I was asking the Lord to release signs, wonders, and miracles during that time. Then I began to daydream about Him again. Suddenly I felt someone grab both my forearms, as if I was going to be pulled somewhere. The grasps were firm and abrupt. I questioned whether this was a holy moment, or whether it was a demonic attack or initiated by unclean spirits.

The Beauty of Jesus | Joma Short

After asking the Holy Spirit, I felt an ease and peace come over me. *Come up here* were the words I heard. I knew I was being taken up to see something, so I yielded my spirit, and up I went.

Two unseen beings grabbed my arms firmly and yanked me up. *This is a bit abrupt*, I thought. But I went along with the leading of the beings. I never saw them, but I soon became acutely aware that they were angels on assignment. I saw some of their outlines. There was one on each side of me. At first, my head began to go into a building and then into a room that was clearly not part of the dimension and realm where I was accustomed to living. My head seemed to be stuck inside the floor, and all I could do was look around and move my eyes. I was in an amazing-looking hallway. Then I was standing on the floor. I just stood there, because I did not know where I was going or what lay at the end of this long hallway. I had come up into the hallway from below the floor, which is a lot different than walking in and out of a door like I am accustomed to doing in the earth realm.

The corridor was beautiful. The floor was burgundy in color. There were marble- or pearl-looking pillars every few yards. The angels began to lead me down the hallway. We walked a long while, and I began to hear sounds. The sounds were that of little people. The sound of children playing and talking began to fill my ears. Finally we came to the entrance of what looked like a large amphitheater. There was stadium-style seating, and each row was full of children. They were all playing or chatting, some held teddy bears or toys, and they all seemed to be waiting for an event or meeting to start.

I was fascinated as I began to walk into the room—but *boom!* As I tried to step into the room, my face hit an invisible barrier. I was surprised by the restraint. The angels did not say anything to me, but I knew in my spirit that I was not allowed to go into that space, yet for some reason I realized I was there by appointment. I needed to see the room, but I did not have access to go into it at that time. My face and body hit the force field with such impact that I had to regain myself. My nose and face actually hurt.

I looked around and wondered what was happening. The angels communicated to my spirit that these were children who had been aborted. The Lord and His servants are caring for them and teaching them up there. I did not know this at the time, but years later, I would go toe-to-toe with Satan in intercession over this upcoming generation of messengers and deliverers.

Jesus has taken the time to add on to His city amphitheaters, housing, and various other buildings to properly care for these young ones. How fascinating. This wasn't part of His plan for the human race—for people to murder their own children—but He takes care of them and gathers them into His house to teach them His ways. Psalm 27:10 says this: "When my father and mother forsake me, the LORD will take care of me." The Lord gathers the children, and despite all their enemies, He brings them into His house.

After seeing portions of this section of His holy city, I began to sink back down into my body. I was back in my dorm room, lying on my couch. *Interesting*, I thought. *Lord, Your city is amazing, and Your heart is so kind. You are good, and Your good-*

ness goes far beyond our comprehension. My eyes have seen marvelous things today.

Takeaway

Jesus has many things to show us and share with us. Each and every one of us has been given assignments on this earth, in the realms, and in the ages to come. I believe that part of my assignment has to do with the ending of abortion on the earth and the discipling of children and youth who have lost their parents. Jesus usually shows us things pertaining to our callings.

If you talk to Him, He will begin to share more and more with you about your callings, and He will begin to give you dreams, visions, insights, and encounters based on your capacity and design. Talk to Jesus. If you are bored with prayer, then I assure you, Jesus is not the boring one. Shake off your dust and slumber and seek Him. He has great and mighty things to share with you. And He is far better than any of us know.

Prayer of Impartation

Raise your hands, open your spirit, and receive this prayer blessing.

> *Father, I thank You that You have made each and every one of us on purpose for a purpose. I pray that this generation will engage You on deeper levels of their purpose, as well as in their individual callings.*
>
> *Lord, I bless this generation and the reader of these words. Lord, strengthen them with might by*

Your Spirit in their inner man. I bless their spirit with strength and might. Lord, I bless them with the spiritual gifts of hunger, thirst, and desire. I know that those who hunger and thirst after You will one day be filled by You!

Lord, I pray that they will not be able to find peace, fulfillment, and satisfaction in other pursuits, passions, or people. Lord, let them lay down their temporary pursuits and may they run into You! You are the Author and the Sustainer of their faith. Father, I bless them with lovesickness. May titles, positions, and jobs mean nothing to them in comparison to their heart and identity as a son or a daughter of the Most High God.

As they gain confidence in You, Lord, reveal to them the deeper things of Your heart. As their heart begins to settle on their identity as a child of God, bring them into greater realms of Your glory. Take them up in the Spirit and show them things that will soon take place.

Lord, remind them that they are living for another age and that You have called them to rule and reign with You in heavenly places.

CHAPTER 3

The Call to Intercession 2005

So I sought for a man among them who would make a wall, and stand in the gap before Me on behalf of the land, that I should not destroy it; but I found no one.

— Ezekiel 22:30

I completed my third year of Bible college, and as a Youth Ministry and Biblical Studies major, I made the commitment to travel and spend my summer serving at different summer camps for teens across the Midwest region of the United States. I knew that my summer was going to be extremely busy, so I wanted to take time in solitude and pursue Jesus intentionally, coupled with prayer and fasting, prior to the summer busyness.

A friend who went to South America to serve and minister for the summer left me the keys to her apartment, and I spent my days of solitude there in her empty place. I exhaled and let the steam and busyness of the school year leave my soul.

Academics, sports, leadership, and my fair share of late-night pranks and social events all came to an end. My week of prayer and fasting had finally begun.

I began to pace the apartment in prayer. I spoke in tongues, and I began to open my spirit to receive from Yahweh. There was no focus or direction to my prayer; I simply opened my spirit and made myself available to Him. I wanted to minister to Him. I wanted to be like Mary and just sit at His feet.

After some time, my worship shifted in its direction. A recurring theme during that season of my life was the book of Joel. So, I was not surprised when the Lord told me to open the book of Joel and "eat it." I was to eat it, digest it, and declare it.

My time of peace and tranquility began to transition into heaviness and sobriety. The Lord reminded me of the urgency of the hour. He also reminded me of my call to intercession. If I was honest with myself, I knew I felt fatigue in that area of my life. Much of what surrounded me in Bible college and the church in which I was serving was not on the same page with me as it pertained to my spiritual walk and the things I was hearing in the secret place.

For some time, I'd had dreams, visions, and encounters surrounding the urgency of the hour, pending and looming catastrophes, and the return of Jesus to the earth. I became so fatigued in the isolation of the battle that I considered toning it down a notch and just becoming a professional pastor. I saw it really wasn't hard to read the Bible, teach, preach, and run events, apart from actually living a life fully surrendered to Jesus. Unfortunately, I saw many pastors and leaders do just that.

In my heart, I was contemplating taking the easy route. That battle and the struggle at times were immense.

As I paced the floor of the apartment, my spirit was finally clean and clear. I was ready to commune with the Lord. I prepared myself for the tough conversations that potentially lay ahead. The Lord continued to remind me of my call to intercession. *I've called you to be an intercessor for this generation,* He said. I remembered and began to weep. Once again, He led me to the book of Joel in the Old Testament. Chapter 2 stood out and was highlighted. I needed to take my place as an intercessor. Though I was not encouraged by the leadership around me at that time of my life, I knew from heaven I was responsible for sounding the alarm, consecrating the assemblies, calling fasts, gathering people, and seeking the Lord. I wrestled with the weight of the call.

Soon my pacing turned to groaning. No longer could I walk or even verbally talk. I began to see a vision. I saw some type of war and bloodshed coming to the cities of our nation. My stomach began to turn because I saw the bodies of young people lying in the streets. Some were just body parts; others were lying there dead. Some type of war and trouble had come to our land. "Lord!" I cried out. "What is this? Am I seeing this correctly?"

The Lord's response shook me to the core of who I was. With His words came the weight of tons of bricks. I felt a force come from heaven and drop into my chest. The weight was so heavy that I fell to the ground and began to groan. His words were this: *Joma, the youth of this nation (the United States of America) will become the world's largest slaughter field or the world's largest harvest field. And intercession is what lays it in the balance.*

When the Lord spoke these words to me, it was as if a thousand-pound load of bricks fell from heaven, and my body crumpled to the ground. A weight rested upon my chest, and a groan began to come from within my soul.

I knew from that point on that, the battle was life or death. If I did not give my vessel over for the purpose of intercession, then the Lord could raise up another. But deliverance for me and my people would not come through my hands. He would raise up another, but I saw the importance of the call. From this point on, if I did not cry out and intercede, then the blood of an entire generation would be on my hands.

> *I sought for a man among them who would make a wall, and stand in the gap before Me on behalf of the land, that I should not destroy it; but I found no one.*
>
> — Ezekiel 22:30

The wailing and groaning led to full-blown travail. Waves of prayer gripped my entire being. An invisible weight rested upon me to the point that I couldn't get off the floor, so I dragged a mattress off of the bunk bed and lay upon it for hours under the weight of intercession. From afternoon all the way into evening, I wailed, crying out for mercy and a harvest of souls. Can a nation be birthed in a day? Can a nation be saved? "Awakening!" I cried those words again and again until I had no more strength in my body. I cried out all my hydration. Blood vessels broke all over my face and neck. Sometime in the night, I finally fell asleep.

When I woke up, I was surprised to see it was morning. I wasn't sure when I had fallen asleep, but after going into the bathroom, I saw my face and how disfigured it had become. My eyes were almost swollen shut. Wow! I didn't dare go out in public looking like this anytime soon. Thank God I was able to stay alone in prayer and fasting for a few more days. I knew after that encounter, I would never be the same again. Indeed, it took a few days for my face to heal and go back to a somewhat normal appearance.

As I began to journal everything that had happened, in my heart I said yes: Yes to a life of intercession. Yes to a life of following Jesus' lead and not being concerned about what others say ministry is or what ministry should look like. I asked the Lord for help, guidance, and leadership. I said yes to the call, but I also knew I needed someone who could help lead and mentor me on this journey. To date, I hadn't met anyone who spoke the same language as me. Nor was I truly encouraged to walk into the fullness of the things that Jesus had revealed to me in the secret place. So, I said yes to the call of intercession. "But, Lord," I pleaded, "please give me a mentor."

As quickly as I asked, He said, *Bickle.*

What? "Lord, now is not the time for jokes. This is serious stuff. Did You just say 'pickle'?!"

Bickle, He said again. *You need to be where this person is.*

I knew then that "Bickle" was the name of a person. I had never heard of anyone by that name before, even during all my international travels. But I knew in my heart that Bickle was the mentor I needed. I didn't feel led to seek this person out, especially since I had already made commitments to travel and help lead summer camps across the Midwest.

Also, I was almost done with my four-year college degree program and on my way to becoming a licensed minister. I wrote down the name, and I knew in my heart that once I came across someone by that name, it would be time for me to relocate to wherever they were.

Ever since that day of travailing intercession, I've been a different person. Something from heaven was deposited deep inside my spirit, and I carry it around in my chest and in my belly. I also have an inner brokenness and sobriety inside me that causes me to live a life of vigilance and prayer.

Later in this book, in chapter 7, I will explain what happened when I came across the person named Bickle.

Takeaway

If you are alive right now, then Jesus wants you to be part of this transitional generation. The reality is, you were not made for days of peace; you were made for days of war. The earth and the evil kingdoms of darkness are going to rage, but we must take our place as children of God on the wall of intercession for this generation.

Intercession, prayer, and prophetic decrees are what govern the universe. Nothing is too difficult. Nothing is impossible for the people of God. We must rise to the occasion, get over our own selfishness, and take responsibility for the wars that rage around us. My life is meant for intercession for this generation of youth.

What will your life stand for? Will you let the enemy—both natural and physical—come in and destroy? Or will you contend for this generation and its destiny? Every baby, every child, every teenager alive today is a dream of the King's heart.

Prayer of Impartation

Raise your hands, open your spirit, and receive this prayer of blessing.

Lord, I raise my hands and bless this generation with peace, protection, and provision. As the enemy and his camps rage against this generation, I pray that You will bless them and keep them. Keep their hearts, minds, and souls pure before You.

I ask that You open their eyes to see You as You truly are. I ask that all the plans of diversion and perversion from the enemy be thwarted. I pray that the conscience of this generation would be protected. I pray for the United States of America. Lord, I pray that war does not come on our land again, but I know that much repentance is still needed. The United States is drunk off the blood of over sixty million murdered babies. And I know that You are true and righteous altogether.

Like Abraham Lincoln said, "The judgments of the Lord are true and righteous all together." In reference to the Civil War and the injustice of the slaves and the innocent bloodshed of the Africans, he knew the arduous Civil War would continue until Your justice was satisfied with the equal number of Americans who would die in the Civil War equal to the number of slaves who were unjustly murdered in their captivity. Lord, have mercy! I plead the blood of Jesus over my sins and over the sins of my nation. God, end the scourge of abortion and send revival to America.

I pray that instead of judgment, You would send mercy. I use my voice as a trumpet calling for gatherings of repentance and prayer. Father, sound the alarm over this generation. I proclaim that we must seek the Lord while there is still yet time.

CHAPTER 4

Power Encounters

Finally, my brethren, be strong in the Lord and in the power of His might.

— Ephesians 6:10

After taking my place as an intercessor for this generation, I became a different person in the spirit. It was as though the spiritual realms, and even the natural realms, knew I was one who carried the seed of promise. I began to encounter the angelic and the demonic in a way I had never experienced before.

I believe that day on the apartment floor I went toe-to-toe with Satan himself over this generation. And I believe I won. In the exchange that took place as I stood in the gap for an entire generation, I laid down my life to the extent that I was willing to do whatever it took to snatch as many as possible from the grasp of the evil one—even to the extent of laying down my own life.

Now I needed to go forward and take possession of everything that already rightfully belonged to Jesus. The battle was won. There were other times of travailing prayer when I addressed Satan over this generation, and those days were other turning points in the Spirit as well.

For the next year and a half, I went into a season of living under an intense open heaven. I believe some of my running mates and friends experienced the same thing as well. The window of time between 2005 and 2007 became monumental and transitional years for my life. I will share a few encounters that shifted the course of my life during this season of personal open heavens. Honestly, I stepped into a realm of power that I was not yet mature enough to steward.

I believe it was the Lord's wisdom to let me experience these deep things in the Spirit, but as I asked Him to take me on a journey of growth and maturing in life, in the Spirit, and in my heart, He let that time of "crossing over" last only for a season. I know that when the time is right, I will cross back over and be able to sustain that level of glory on a daily basis.

THE BREAKER ANOINTING

While at my mother's house on a break from a summer of ministry and travels, as usual I spent time in study and prayer in my childhood bedroom. The times of prayer and intimacy with the Lord there in my childhood bedroom were rich. As I spent time with the Lord, I added a few days of fasting on top of the prayers. One night as I laid my head down to go to sleep for the night, I felt the climate of my room begin to change.

The enemy must have been threatened by all my breakthroughs in prayer, because as I began to rest my soul and prepare to go to sleep, I felt a shift in the room. But this was not a good shift. The temperature of the room became very hot. My face was turned toward a wall, but I felt the presence of pure evil standing behind me and I saw a red glare bouncing off the wall in front of me. Within myself, I wasn't sure I wanted to turn around. I did not know what type of creature would be standing there. Whatever it was, I knew it came from a very dark place. I'm not sure if it knew whether I was awake or asleep.

I lay there very still, talking to Holy Spirit, deciding what to do next. The longer I waited, the more the room became illuminated with a red-and-orange-colored light. I angled my head enough to see where the color was coming from. The vanity mirror that attached to my bedroom dresser had transformed into a portal. The best I can describe is that it looked like a portal from hell had opened in my bedroom. I saw fiery flames coming from within the portal. I heard the distant voices of people or creatures on the other side of the portal.

I thought to myself, *My God, what has come to mess with me tonight? And why did it come to me? Hmmm. I must be about to enter into something that is a threat to the kingdom of darkness. Well, I am not going to give into these demonstrative tactics of fear.* I lay there a few more moments, building myself up from within in my most holy faith. I had to remind myself who I was before I took my next step. I finally decided to face this giant. This principality from hell had had the nerve to come into my bedroom—and if it was a fight that it wanted, then a fight it would get.

Boom. I turned around, wielding my sword of the Spirit. Praying in tongues, I abruptly turned around and lunged at the entity. As I turned, it was as if it had been waiting for me to respond, and it immediately lunged back at me. We fought and wrestled in my bedroom that night. We tossed to and fro on my bed, hit the wall, then fell back on the bed again. A supernatural power from heaven came from within me, and I felt invincible. I yelled and wrestled like one who could not be defeated. Finally, filled with faith, I experienced a surge of power with a mighty flash of light—and then, *boom*. I finally prevailed. The prince of darkness was bound. He lost, he vanished, and the portal closed.

Pheewww... an eerie peace and silence were left in the room. The color changed from red-hot flames to cool blues and smoky grays. All my senses were heightened. I knew, just from listening, that my mother was awake in the room next door. I think she was hesitant to check on me, not knowing what she'd find. She'd heard the struggle and some of the battle, but I am sure the presence of evil might have scared her or anyone else who was awake.

As I lay on my bed considering what had just happened, I began to open my mouth and sing. The most eerily beautiful song began to come out of my mouth. I sang a song in the Spirit. A song came forth from a deep place in the heavenlies. It was a song in the Spirit, in a tongue I had never heard before or heard since. As I sang out, a cleansing hovered throughout my room, and then it moved into every room in the house. A heavenly peace shifted the atmosphere of the entire home. The shift was so evident that even outside my home, the neighborhood became silent, with not one noise from a person, an animal, or even a vehicle.

I learned later that the feeling of peace was so strong, it put my mother into a deep sleep. I transitioned from a war-type mode to a more peaceful state as well. But I was no longer tired. I was full of energy from the supernatural deposits and exchanges. So I left my room to go get some water and use the restroom. To my surprise, as I touched the door handle to my room, it fell apart. I tried to simply twist the door handle, but it broke and even fell out of the mount in the door. *Wow, strange!* I thought. Then I walked to the bathroom a few doors away. I went to sit down, and the toilet seat broke. *Whoa… what is going on?* I tried to stabilize the seat, and the seat broke completely off the rest of the toilet. I tried to wash my hands, and the faucet broke! Water began to spray up out of the pipe! *Okay, I get it now.* There is some power resting on me at the moment, and I shouldn't touch anything else. So I slowly turned off the water valves and lay back down in bed.

Wow. How am I going to explain all of the broken things to my mother? I do not know. But I thought to myself, *I wonder if some of this has to do with the "Breaker Anointing." Lord, help me steward this gift.*

Takeaway

As we continue to approach the day of the Lord's return, we are going to face more frequent interactions with other realms and dimensions. Humankind on planet earth is going to reach levels of darkness and depravity such as the world has never seen or experienced before. Jesus Himself said that the day of the coming of the Lord would be much like the days of Noah.

Depravity, wickedness, and the interbreeding of wickedness will reach its fullness. But the Lord is raising up a people who will be able to contend with the darkness, the demon worship, the aliens, the sorcery, and the hybrid races. We must learn the weapons of our warfare. We have no time to waste.

The enemy and his armies are not sitting idly by. The mainstream church world is far behind the tide when it comes to spiritual warfare and actually walking in our authority as children of God. We must prepare ourselves now so that we are not led astray or infiltrated in the future.

If we are children of God, then we are going to need to rise up to the level of our birthright. As children of God, we are called to rule the universe with Him. And I will take it a step further: As followers of *Yeshua Ha Messiach*, Jesus the Christ, we need to outgrow our religious and petty differences. All of creation is groaning and waiting for the manifestation of the sons of God in the earth, and the Western church is too busy arguing about doctrine and holding bake sales and bingo nights. As a mother in the faith, and a mother in the Spirit, I say to you, it is time to grow up and grow into our birthright as children of God.

It should not be the case that witches, warlocks, New Agers, Luciferians, the Illuminati, and others who practice in the occult should operate in realms and dimensions of power that are greater than that of the family of Almighty God.

Prayer of Impartation

Raise your hands, open your spirit, and receive this prayer of blessing and impartation.

> *Father, I bless this generation with the hope of their calling in Messiah Jesus. I bless them with knowing the awesome and creative weapons of their warfare.*

Father, show them that Jesus is not only their Living Hope, but He is the desire of every living thing.

Father, I bless them with confidence, worth, and identity. I ask that You open Your Word to them and reveal the weapons of their warfare. Take them on a journey of utilizing their spiritual weapons. Take them into the deeper things of God. Lord, sharpen their discernment, and draw them deeper into Your beauty. Lord, reveal the authority that comes from knowing You and walking not only as the bride of Christ, but also as sons of God.

MOSES AND ELIJAH— CROSSING OVER THE THIN VEIL

Now after six days Jesus took Peter, James, and John his brother, led them up on a high mountain by themselves; and He was transfigured before them. His face shone like the sun, and His clothes became as white as the light. And behold, Moses and Elijah appeared to them, talking with Him. Then Peter answered and said to Jesus, "Lord, it is good for us to be here; if You wish, let us make here three tabernacles: one for You, one for Moses, and one for Elijah."

While he was still speaking, behold, a bright cloud overshadowed them; and suddenly a voice came out of the cloud, saying, "This is My beloved Son, in whom I am well pleased. Hear Him!" And when the disciples heard it, they fell on their faces and were greatly afraid. But Jesus came and touched them and said, "Arise, and do not be afraid." When they had lifted up their eyes, they saw no one but Jesus only.

Now as they came down from the mountain, Jesus commanded them, saying, "Tell the vision to no one until the Son of Man is risen from the dead."

— Matthew 17:1–9

Another power encounter I experienced reminded me of this "breaker" type of anointing and power. I was back in my dorm room at this point during my junior year of college. My roommate was sound asleep in the bunk beneath me while I lay wide awake on the top bunk. During this season of life, I was meditating on the books of Revelation, Zechariah, and Jeremiah. An intensified urgency for preparing for the end of times and the end of the age began to consume my devotional times and personal studies.

While lying on the bed, I began to slip into another realm again. The room filled with lights and colors of whites that carried a different type of depth and dimension. I transitioned into the other realm; it was as if the earthly realm and my dorm room disappeared into another dimension yet I still lay on my bed. Then I saw and heard two men talking loudly while shaking their hands in the air. They had papers and scrolls—plans and assignments—in their arms. They were preparing for the end of the age. I just knew it in my spirit. Heaven was busy making preparations.

The New Jerusalem was busy. I saw long, tall creatures that seemed like angels; they were definitely not people. They were busy making these absolutely beautiful garments. They were making them and folding them, then putting them away with great care into wardrobes. The Scripture went through my head: "The righteous acts of the saints. And you will be clothed with garments." What an honor! These creatures are making garments for the people of God. Revelation 19:8 states, "And to her it was granted to be arrayed in fine linen, clean and bright, for the fine linen is the righteous acts of the saints." These creatures were busy preparing garments for the saints on the earth.

Then the two men who were there "discussing" matters, in standard loud and demonstrative Middle Eastern fashion, looked over at me, but they continued doing what they were doing. No one said a word to me. My spirit knew they were Moses and Elijah. I closely watched what they were doing, yet they never said a word to me. They were speaking loudly in a language that I did not understand, and it almost felt to me like they were arguing, but the longer I listened, I realized they were just passionate Middle Eastern men having discussions about the scrolls in their hands and how they were going to aid in accomplishing the mission. They had many scrolls in their hands.

I stayed in that realm for a while, but to my surprise, no one said anything specifically to me. I just felt the energy and was awed by the dimensions and the absolute busyness taking place in the New Jerusalem. I knew they were busy preparing for the end of the age, and I needed to do the same. They were doing their part, so I needed to do my part too. The entire experience was humbling, and it left me with an awed sense of sobriety in my spirit.

After some time, I transitioned back into the earthly realm, but when I did, an electrifying power came back with me. The angelic realm was in my bedroom as well, and the magnitude of the weight was a bit terrifying. I tried to wake up my roommate, but she was snoring, out like a light. Then I let out a little scream, because I saw a scroll rolled out before my face and someone told me to take it and eat it. I said, "No." There was writing on the front and the back. I could not understand the words on the scroll, but I knew it had to do with "Eat the scroll and it will be sweet to your taste but sour to your stomach. You will go and prophesy to kings and queens, and dignitaries... You will prophesy to many nations" (see Ezekiel 3:1–4).

Revelation 10: 8-11 states, "Then the voice which I heard from heaven spoke to me again and said, 'Go, take the little book which is open in the hand of the angel who stands on the sea and on the earth.' So I went to the angel and said to him, 'Give me the little book.' And he said to me, 'Take and eat it; and it will make your stomach bitter, but it will be as sweet as honey in your mouth.' Then I took the little book out of the angel's hand and ate it, and it was as sweet as honey in my mouth. But when I had eaten it, my stomach became bitter. And he said to me, 'You must prophesy again about many peoples, nations, tongues, and kings.'"

Then I saw a *beautiful tree*. It looked like an almond tree, and next to Jesus, it was the most beautiful sight I have ever seen. One specific branch of the tree was sparkling and illuminated with dazzling light and glory. It was the Branch of the Lord.

I wanted to know what I was getting into before I said yes, under the weight of this Presence. I did not understand everything that was happening, and I did not want to be held accountable to the scroll if I did not know what it said or what it fully meant. (I later repented for saying no—years later.)

As the scroll was rolling and the encounter was ending, I felt a surge of power again. But my room could not handle the transition. By this time, it was the middle of the night. Everything was normally still at that time, but then the electrical outlets began to fry. The hair dryer went off and then blew out. The alarm clock began to ring. The phone began to ring, though no one was calling. The microwave was short-circuited. I thought to myself, *Lord, send help! Everything is breaking!*

My vision at that point became more developed. At night, as I began to lay down and wind down from the day, I began to see into the spirit realm. I began to see the New Jerusalem, and sometimes went other places. Other times I stayed put and saw things.

Takeaway

As human beings, we have been made in the image of the Lord. We are three parts, much like He is triune, meaning that Yahweh is a three-part Person and we relate to Him as Father, Son/Yeshua/Jesus, and Holy Spirit. As humans, we are spiritual beings, who have a soulish realm, but we live in an earthly body. As we grow and mature, we need to become acquainted with ourselves—spirit, soul, and body. First Thessalonians 5:23 says, "Now may the God of peace Himself sanctify you completely; and may your whole spirit, soul, and body be preserved blameless at the coming of our Lord Jesus Christ."

As we grow and mature in Christ, a sanctifying process happens in which our spirits, souls, and bodies are all made whole as we are transformed day by day into His image. This is why it is so important to spend our days beholding Jesus. Not only is He the Author and Perfecter of our faith, but He is committed to our beautifying and sanctification process.

As we become more like Him, we are able to learn to steward and govern ourselves and take our place of authority in the spirit realms. The New Jerusalem is a very busy place. Moses, Elijah, angels, other creatures, and saints who have gone before us are busy preparing for the day of Jesus' return to the earth. It is not fitting for us as believers here in the earth realm to be lazy or unengaged with the very theme and storyline of the New Jerusalem. If they are busy about the Father's business, then we need to be busy about His business as well.

The reality is, He has scrolls of destiny written for each of our lives. It is not only our responsibility to receive our scroll(s), but it is also our responsibility to be diligent and faithful about carrying them out. Scrolls of destiny and assignments in this realm are directly connected to other realms as well. I will not go into much detail here about all the heavenly resources that we possess, but the reality is, that King Jesus has provided everything we need to accomplish our missions in the earth. His provision is not only for our physical goods, finances, and health. He has also provided spiritual resources. We have spiritual gifts and spiritual weapons that many are familiar with, but there is more. Yahweh also gave us realms and dimensions of power we can create. We as humans have an arch, stars, angels, mountains, weapons, and more assigned to our lives.

The veil between the natural and the spiritual is much thinner than most of us believe. There is a very thin veil that separates the spiritual realm and the physical, earthly realm. Just like Jesus said about the Holy Spirit—the wind blows, and you do not see it, but you feel its effects—so it is with the spiritual realm. You may not always see it, but every day you will feel its effects.

John 3:8 says, "The wind blows where it wishes, and you hear the sound of it, but cannot tell where it comes from and where it goes. So is everyone who is born of the Spirit." There is a power in which we as the children of God are destined to walk. We need to learn to steward everything that has been given to us, not just for the sake of ourselves, but for the sake of all of creation. The reality is that Satan and the other fallen ones are working overtime to pervert, steal, corrupt, and misuse what Jesus gave us as blood-bought humans in His sovereignty.

Let us take back our rightful authority in the Spirit and begin to rule and reign again in heavenly places. Many of us have great power and gifts—we only need to be given permission to step into them. This is your time. Permission is granted to you from the Father!

In a few years, people will be operating in such levels of darkness that they can change weather patterns, move from place to place, change elements and shape-shift, perform demonic wonders and miracles, and much more. Where will the people of God be in that day? Who will stand against them? Who will be some of the mighty witnesses for the Lord?

Not everyone will rise to the occasion, but some will. Are you one of those? During the last three and a half years before

Jesus comes back to the earth, there will be groups of witnesses all over the earth who will operate in a power greater than anything the darkness can muster up. The power will be greater than that of Moses and Elijah and the power that rested on the early church combined.

Leadership during those days will take years of preparation. So, go ahead and start now. It is time to grow and accelerate into the deeper things of God. It is time to learn to govern and steward the earth. All of creation is groaning and waiting for the revealing of the sons of God in the earth. Are you satisfied with just playing church games and attending weak services and prayer meetings? Or are you going to transition into your birthright and begin to speak and create at the same level as Jesus Himself?

Prayer of Impartation

If you are ready and wanting to take your spiritual walk to the next level, then raise your hands, open your spirit, and receive this blessing.

> *Father, in the mighty name of Messiah Jesus, I bless this dear reader with spiritual might, fortitude, and governing power. You, Lord Jesus, are our King, and everything that belongs to You now belongs to us. Every weapon, every recourse, and every amount of provision is now ours. I speak forth a breaking in of light, power, and might. I pray that You reveal Your-*

self as Adonai Perazim, the Lord who breaks out in
the midst of His people.

I ask that You open the Living Word, the Bible, to
this reader and give fresh revelation and new insight
into Your Word. I thank You that the entrance of your
Word brings light. And Your light divides even soul
and spirit. I pray that the children of God in the earth
are emboldened to take their place and rise in authori-
ty in their regions, lands, locations, and dimensions.

Over the children of God in this hour, I pray for
freedom from religion, works of the flesh, and the tra-
ditions of men. I speak forth a deposit from heaven for
the sake of Your unveiling. Cause your children to come
forth! It is time for them to come forth! They were born
for such a time as this.

SHINING IN THE
NIGHT

Another account of power where some of the Lord's glory was displayed in a uniquely tangible fashion happened at a retreat for high school students. I was a leader for a group of about twelve teenage girls from rougher places in life. The retreat lasted for three days, and we spent overnights in hotel-type dorm rooms. By the last night of the retreat, the girls had gained a special liking for me, and they began to ask me more about my personal life.

We were back in our room and getting ready to settle in for the night. I already turned all the lights out in our room as we had a 10 p.m. lights-out rule. But as you can imagine, all the girls were still talking and chitchatting about the day and all our activities. I happened to be reading my Bible from John chapter 10 when they interrupted me to ask more questions about my life. So, I told them about Jesus and how He was my first love and my Shepherd. Because they were teenage girls from turbulent backgrounds, they did not know much about the Bible or Jesus. Most of them began to ask me about boys and romance and whether I was dating anyone. I told them I was not dating, and I began to expound on how and why I had intentionally set myself apart for the Lord during this season of my life.

I shared how we only have a short time on this earth so we should give Him our singleness and our youth, and I wanted to give Him the strength of my youth. I wanted Jesus to have all of me for my young adult years. I then told them that if and when He desired me to open my eyes and heart to marriage, then He would let me know. They were intrigued. They had never met a pretty and talented lady like myself who was not only a virgin, but also who did not want to date.

They then began to ask about the Bible, and as they asked their questions, I began to explain creation, salvation, and the love of God. A few of the girls began to gasp. Others began to cry. A few of the girls began to scream. "What is wrong?" I asked. I thought maybe one of them needed deliverance, because at times I had experienced that as I began to share the Gospel with an unbeliever, they began to manifest demons in various ways. At times when people began manifesting demons, they were not aware of how to regain control of their bodies. But this was different. Some of the girls came close to my face, while others ran back away from me. "What is going on?!" I asked again.

One of the girls said, "You're glowing! There's light coming out of your eyes! Your skin is sparkling and shining!" "Oh, really?" I asked. *Wow.* Then I explained to them that it was a sign to them that what I was saying was the truth. I told them how powerful Jesus is and how He is full of light, and those who love Him are also full of light. Psalm 34:5 says, "Those who look to him are radiant; their faces are never covered in shame" (NIV). The young ladies began to acknowledge the glowing as a miracle. Some of them were still scared, but others wept quietly and said they wanted to know Jesus in a personal way. They confessed they'd never heard words like these before.

Takeaway

The words of Daniel and the life of Moses stood out to me concerning this occurrence. Daniel 12:3 states, "Those who are [spiritually] wise will shine brightly like the brightness of the expanse of heaven, and those who lead many to righteousness, [will shine] like the stars forever and ever" (amp).

After spending time with the Lord and encountering Him on the mountain, Moses came back down to speak with the people, and as he did, his face glowed with the glory of God:

> *Now it was so, when Moses came down from Mount Sinai (and the two tablets of the Testimony were in Moses' hand when he came down from the mountain), that Moses did not know that the skin of his face shone while he talked with Him. So when Aaron and all the children of Israel saw Moses, behold, the skin of*

his face shone, and they were afraid to come near him. Then Moses called to them, and Aaron and all the rulers of the congregation returned to him; and Moses talked with them. Afterward all the children of Israel came near, and he gave them as commandments all that the LORD had spoken with him on Mount Sinai. And when Moses had finished speaking with them, he put a veil on his face. But whenever Moses went in before the LORD to speak with Him, he would take the veil off until he came out; and he would come out and speak to the children of Israel whatever he had been commanded. And whenever the children of Israel saw the face of Moses, that the skin of Moses' face shone, then Moses would put the veil on his face again, until he went in to speak with Him."

— Exodus 34:29–35 NKJV

The Lord is the same. Our eternal Jesus is the same yesterday, today, and forever. He does not change, nor does He consider people from the Bible days to be more important to Him than those of us living on the earth today. Because I valued Him, and because I took my relationship with Him seriously and my desire was to speak with Him face-to-face even as a friend speaks to a friend, there was a measure of glory that rested upon my life.

The shining of my face and eyes testified to His goodness in the lives of those teenage girls on a cold, dark night in Minnesota. In the mundane life of a youth leader and mentor for troubled youth, the glory of God shined through. If He did that through me, then how much more can He do through you?

Prayer of Impartation

Raise your hands, open your spirit man, and receive this prayer of importation and blessing.

Lord, I thank You for the receiver of this prayer. I pray that You would bless them with the gift of spiritual thirst and spiritual hunger. I pray that the things that once satisfied their souls will become stale and dissatisfying. I pray they will have an insatiable desire for Your Presence.

I ask that You make them like Joshua, the son of Nun, who never wanted to leave the manifestation of Your glory in the Tent of Meeting. Make them ones who value Your Presence above all else. I pray that as they seek You, they will run into Your heavy glory. Let them experience Your weighty glory that is beyond our comprehension. Let the weight of Your glory so come into their space that all they can do is fall down and receive and behold Your goodness.

As they arise, let unusual and mighty miracles be done in and through them. Your Word says that those who look to You are radiant (Psalm 34:5). I pray that You shine the light of Your face on them. May they feel the heat and the intensity of Your gaze. Lord, let Your glory shine to them and through them. I ask these things in the almighty name of Jesus, our Messiah. Amen!

CHAPTER 5

The Call to Israel

For Zion's sake I will not hold My peace,
And for Jerusalem's sake I will not rest,
Until her righteousness goes forth as brightness,
And her salvation as a lamp that burns.

— Isaiah 62:1

L eading into the year 2006, I became aware that my life was on a trajectory with the Lord that I had no grid or paradigm to perceive. Though I mostly completed my four-year bachelor's degree in Pastoral Studies, and I was only months away from receiving my minister's license, I felt the Lord calling me away. There was a pulling in my spirit to follow the Lord into the unknown. The pull was so strong that some days it baffled me. I thought becoming a youth pastor and ministering both nationally and internationally was what Jesus had appointed me to do in life. Did I miss something major along the way? I felt deep down inside there was something amiss in my understanding, and my spirit was aware of it.

In my personal times of prayer, I heard Him tell me, *I am going to smash all your paradigms about your life and what ministry looks like.* All the man-made ideas, religion, job titles, and rhetoric—what I believed ministry looked like—He was about to shatter. I began to wonder if the past three and a half years of my life were useless and if I had wasted my time in vain working toward a ministerial degree. If I was not called to minister in this way, then had I made a mistake in going to Bible college? Should I even finish? I did not have any "next step" from Him, so I just continued to fulfill my commitments to complete my degree, but I began to hold everything very loosely.

In the secret places of prayer and devotion, I laid my life on the altar once again. "Lord, do what You want with me," was my daily prayer. "I give everything over to You once again. You can erase all the whiteboards of my life and my life plans. Lord, take me and do what You desire to do with my life."

I began to pray and fast and ask Him to reveal to me my life's calling. One night as I lay down to sleep, the Lord caught me up in a vision. I was taken over this beautiful city. It had building structures and architecture like I had never seen before in the entirety of my existence. I wondered if maybe I was seeing into the past. But the longer I looked, the more I realized I was seeing in real time. As I hovered over the city, I began to fall in love with the land and the layout.

As I looked out at the rooftops of these stone buildings, people began to hang cloth from some of the windows. The people were beautiful, and the cloths were deep purple and gold. I continued to stare at the beautiful cityscape, loving every sight and sound. *What a beautiful and special place,* I thought. I held the encounter in my heart. I was not sure where I was seeing, but knew it was home. Something about this city called out to me. It felt in my spirit like we were made for one another, and I knew this was the place of my inheritance.

A week later, I was praying and waiting on the Lord, and He took me up into the heavenlies with Him again. Other than the encounter I described in Chapter 1, this was the only time when the Lord took me awake into the heavens in this way. This time He took me up into the clouds. We did not go up into the highest heavens, but He took me to where He was at the moment. We were somewhere that seemed to me like the second heavens. There were stars and thin clouds around us. There in the darkness, He was sitting. He didn't say anything. He just sat there. I don't know of anyone who just sits there suspended in the middle of the air, but He did. And as He sat there, seemingly thinking deeply, I just copied Him and sat beside Him. I followed His lead. He is my favorite human. I absolutely adore Him. I was just happy that He had brought me up for a visit. My heart's desire was to be close to Him, and oftentimes during the day, I would stop and ask Jesus where He was and what He was doing. I just wanted to be with Him and stay near Him.

I expected Jesus to begin talking and tell me something especially significant, but instead of talking, we just sat in silence for a long time. He looked at me once or twice, but He did not initiate a conversation. We just sat there, suspended in a different dimension and angle than what was familiar to me. I noticed His gaze was fixed on something. He didn't break His gaze from this location for a very long time. Since His eyes were fixed on it, I looked over in curiosity at what had captured

His attention. I wondered what He was staring at and why He was staring so intently.

As I looked and followed the line of sight from His gaze, the clouds parted, and I saw His eyes were fixed on a particular plot of land. I saw an aerial view of these lands. There was something special about this plot of land, but it also did not look familiar to me.

There was a time when Jesus and I had hovered over part of Africa and maybe Australia as well, but this area and region was different. Africa was going to be a place of refuge, shelter, and abundance. I saw rolling fields of fertile vegetation growing and over abounding providence and provision coming from the rich lands of African soil. The sight was absolutely beautiful and rich. There was going to be a sound and a shout of praise coming from Africa and Australia as well. I looked forward to seeing these things come to fruition in the days ahead. In the days to come, these lands are going to be key to the end time harvest. There will be safety and provision found in these places while there is chaos and destruction in other parts of the world.

But this plot of land He was currently looking at was a different kind of special. It was set apart in a different way. It was not Africa or Australia. It was His. After some time, I went back into my body, and then I was back at home. I pondered on all these things. What was this land He kept staring at and showing me from the clouds? Why did this land matter so much to Him, and why did He spend so much time thinking and planning concerning it?

As I went to work the next day, I spent my lunch period waiting on the Lord and pondering everything that had happened the night before. As I sat and communed with the Holy Spirit, I began to receive insight from an angel. The angel gave me a name that caused me to look up where that name came from. I thought it might be associated with the land I had seen the night before. I discovered the name was associated with an ancient people group. As I read more information about them online, out of nowhere, an image came across my screen. The image was exactly what I had seen the night before in the clouds with Jesus! It was even the exact same angle and image! I was so shocked when I saw the image that I actually fell out of my chair at work. I was knocked right out of my chair. Something holy was happening. I shut the door to my office area and asked the Lord for help. I found the image details and saved it to my computer. I then looked up the photo credits and who had captured the photo. To my amazement, I discovered an astronaut had taken the image *the night before*, at the *exact same time* when I was with Jesus in the heavenlies! This photo was a confirmation that was captured in the natural of everything that had happened when I was in the Spirit with Jesus in the second heavens. This photo was a tangible image of what I had seen and the place where Jesus' gaze was intently fixed.

In complete amazement, I zoomed in on the photos and realized the images were of the Fertile Crescent and the Holy Land of Israel. As the photographer zoomed in closer, I saw the buildings and structures of the land and not just the aerial view from out in space. To my amazement, these were the very buildings I'd seen in my vision the week before! Those beautiful stone buildings I had seen were located in Jerusalem, Israel. I began to weep, and weep, and weep, and weep.

A love and desire for His land and His people overtook me. This was my calling. I was called to partner with Him for Israel. Just like we had sat and gazed at the aerial view of the land, I knew I was to partner with Him for His purposes in that beautiful place. He was praying and strategizing. I remember loving Him as He gazed. As He gazed at the land, I remember wondering what was on His mind. He fascinated me. There, sobbing in my office while kneeling on the floor, I said *yes* to partnering with His heart for this special land.

After that day of weeping, a supernatural deposit of love for Israel entered my soul and my spirit. I began to acknowledge a personal calling to the land of Israel. I had never been aware of a calling to that part of the world before. It all felt so new. I felt as if the entire trajectory of my life was now changing. I did not know how to even make such a major course correction at this point in life. So I laid myself on the altar once again. My prayer was simple and honest: "Lord, if You are calling me to go to Israel, then make a way for me to go. I have no plans, connections, or even resources of my own to get me there."

I told no one of my recent encounters. I told no one of my visions of Israel and the newly developed love I had for this land and this people. I cleaned my face of all the tears and kept up with my weekly routines. At this point, I was in my senior year of college and was carrying a full courseload to finish my double major in four years. My major was a combination of Youth Ministry, Pastoral Studies, and Biblical Studies.

To receive a bachelor of arts degree, I needed to pick a foreign language to study. As a freshman, just enrolling for classes about four years prior, I already possessed a strong knowledge of Spanish. I already spoke conversationally and had even led worship in Spanish at times. It seemed natural to just continue on in that language, but for some reason, as I signed up for classes, my heart was pulled toward taking Hebrew. I was shocked by this strong pull toward Hebrew. I had never spoken or even studied a Semitic language before, yet my heart was drawn to it.

So, for the previous three years, I had become a student of biblical Hebrew. I went from being a beginner to thriving and studying in the advanced classes with Bible translators. For assignments we actually translated the original Hebrew text into English. My knowledge of Hebrew opened the Bible up to me in a new and fascinating way. I was grateful for the understanding and revelation that rested upon the language. I liked the classes and continued on with biblical Hebrew even past the required two years, but I did not think much of the acquired skill set other than it being a great Bible study skill and that I had enjoyed the classes.

One weekday after classes were over, I went to my mailbox at the campus mailroom to pick up my mail as usual. I did not receive much mail, so I expected the box to be empty. But to my surprise, when I opened the mailbox, a large envelope had been stuffed inside. I pulled out the package. The envelope was a large, 8½-by-11-inch tan package that seemed to be full of materials. A cover letter was addressed to me, and I was intrigued.

I walked over to a side table and begin to look at the contents more closely. The opening letter read, "Congratulations, Joma! You are the winner of this year's Israel trip!" What? I had not signed up for any trips. I never entered a raffle. I had not even heard of any trips being taken to Israel or the Middle East. I thought, *This is a joke. There must be a mistake.* But the further I read, the more I saw this was a real trip. And I seemingly had just won an all-expense-paid trip to Israel. At the bottom of the letter, I saw it had been signed by a certain professor—the head of our Biblical Languages Department. I thought to myself, *I need to go to his office and see for myself if this is real. I have so many questions!*

I walked most of the way up to the second floor in a daze and entered the hall where his office was located. I figured he might not even be in his office since he was a busy and much-sought-after man. But sure enough, as I walked to the door, there he sat. Before I could even knock, he looked up at me and said, "So, I see you got your package! Congratulations! It is much deserved."

I held up the envelope and said, "So you know about all this?" His response was a laugh. Then he explained about how he had met with all the professors from the Pastoral Studies and Biblical Languages Department. Every year they picked two outstanding seniors who came through either program and showed excellence in academics, character, and knowledge of the Word and biblical language interpretation.

Apparently, I was the unanimous choice made by all the professors. My heart melted at the thought of so many of my professors speaking highly of me behind closed doors. Then, in addition to that, for them to have enough confidence in me to send me to Israel on a full scholarship to experience the Word in His native land? I was undone. I told him I had never applied for anything, and I had not even known about the trip, so I was shocked. But I was so grateful for the honor. He began to shower me with generous words and blessings as a scholar and theologian. He wanted me to go further and gain my master's of divinity for he thought I was a brilliant mind in this generation. I told him I would consider it and pray about those endeavors, but for now I desired to serve young people and disciple them into harvesting the nations. I gave him my profound thanks and walked back to my dorm room.

I walked in what felt like a bubble up the stairs to the fourth floor, where I was living, then gently closed my room door. I sat down on the floor, amazed as I began to look through the packet. I looked at photos of Jerusalem, Tel Aviv, Eliat, and other places around Israel. The pictures were so similar to the vision I had had of the stone buildings. The distinctly beautiful architecture stood out to me once again.

Then I heard the Lord speak. *Do you believe Me now? There. You are going to Israel.* My God! He gave me the call from heaven, and then He made a way for me to get there. I had had no part of the process besides saying yes to Him and loving Him from a place of sincerity. He truly makes our paths straight. Wherever He calls, He leads the way and provides. I spread myself flat on my face on the floor of my dorm room and pondered all these things in my heart. Wow. *Thank You, Lord!*

Takeaway

Jesus greatly desires Jerusalem. Jerusalem is His city. Jerusalem is the city of the Great King, as Psalm 48 says. Jesus has many plans and desires for the nation of Israel. The reality is that we, as believers and lovers of Jesus, are also called to be lovers of Israel and Jerusalem. The calling of being a watchman placed on the walls of Jerusalem is not a calling just for me, but it is a calling for every believer.

Isaiah 62:1–12 states:

"For Zion's sake I will not hold My peace,
And for Jerusalem's sake I will not rest,
Until her righteousness goes forth as brightness,
And her salvation as a lamp that burns.

"The Gentiles shall see your righteousness,
And all kings your glory.
You shall be called by a new name,
Which the mouth of the LORD will name.

"You shall also be a crown of glory
In the hand of the LORD,
And a royal diadem
In the hand of your God.

"You shall no longer be termed Forsaken,
Nor shall your land any more be termed Desolate;
But you shall be called Hephzibah, and your land
Beulah;
For the LORD delights in you,
And your land shall be married.

"For as a young man marries a virgin,
So shall your sons marry you;
And as the bridegroom rejoices over the bride,
So shall your God rejoice over you.

"I have set watchmen on your walls, O Jerusalem;
They shall never hold their peace day or night.
You who make mention of the LORD, do not keep
silent,

"And give Him no rest till He establishes
And till He makes Jerusalem a praise in the earth.

"The LORD has sworn by His right hand
And by the arm of His strength:
'Surely I will no longer give your grain
As food for your enemies;
And the sons of the foreigner shall not drink your new
wine,
For which you have labored.

"'But those who have gathered it shall eat it,
And praise the LORD;
Those who have brought it together shall drink it in
My holy courts.'

"Go through,
Go through the gates!
Prepare the way for the people;
Build up,
Build up the highway!
Take out the stones,
Lift up a banner for the peoples!

"Indeed the LORD has proclaimed
To the end of the world:
'Say to the daughter of Zion,
"Surely your salvation is coming;
Behold, His reward is with Him,
And His work before Him."'

"And they shall call them The Holy People,
The Redeemed of the LORD;
And you shall be called Sought Out,
A City Not Forsaken."

We, as Christians and lovers of Jesus, are to get to know our older brothers and keepers of the covenant, the Hebrew people. Jesus' name in Hebrew is *Yeshua*. In English, His name is literally translated as *Joshua*, meaning "He is the One who saves."

Our calling as believers, members of The Way, is to mature into being two witnesses. Zechariah, the prophet from the Old Testament, tells us the Lord is bringing forth two witnesses who will minister before the Lord of the whole earth. I believe these two witnesses are Jewish believers and Gentile believers. Together we will minister to the Lord and prepare for the transition of the ages. (The topic of the two witnesses is an extensive reality we must understand, but I will write another book that goes into much more detail about this subject matter. The reality of being a witness of Jesus at the end of the age deserves much explanation, and so my book will include Scripture, revelation, power, knowledge, and a contextual framework. That will take time and a lot more space to unveil.)

The necessity for us to embrace our calling to provoke Israel to jealousy (Romans 9–11) so they desire to worship the Messiah and come to His saving knowledge is evident and urgent. As believers in and lovers of Jesus, we must begin to love His people, the Jewish people. When He returns to rule and reign the earth, He will establish His government from His throne and headquarters—in Jerusalem. As Psalm 2 states, "I have installed my king on Zion, my holy mountain" (NIV).

Our enemy and adversary knows of Jesus' covenant with Israel, and how He will not return again until they call out to Him, "Blessed is He who comes in the name of the Lord." There must be a remnant of Hebrew-speaking believers in the land of Israel to whom He will return. As Jacob's trouble comes again, Israel will not stand alone. But every believer should stand with them, for His people have become our people, and their God is our God. Yeshua is Yahweh. He is the God of Abraham, Isaac, and Jacob. Our prayer is that the blinders would be moved from their eyes, and that the Lord will establish David's tent, which has fallen, both in the Jewish nation as well as in the Gentile nations. We must stand before the Lord of the whole earth and minister to Him together, bringing forth that golden oil.

Prayer of Impartation

Now raise your hands, quiet your spirit, and receive this prayer of blessing and importation.

Father of glory, give Your people the Spirit of wisdom and revelation in the knowledge of who You are. You are holy. You are full of wonder, and You keep all Your promises. You are the Lord of the harvest, who keeps all Your covenants. You, O Lord, are the First and the Last. I ask that You cause Your face to shine upon this dear reader.

Lord, let Your glory rest upon them. As they spend more time with You and get to know You on an intimate level, let them fall in love with Your brethren, the Hebrew people. For that which we have done to the least of these, Your Hebrew people, Your brethren—that we have done to You also. Lord, let Your jealous love melt their heart and impart the same love that You have for the Hebrew people into this dear reader's heart, mind, and spirit.

May the receiver of this prayer take his or her place as a watchman on the wall of intercession for Your Hebrew people. May the oneness in the Messiah be made manifest in and through us. Lord, we call for the One New Man in the Messiah. Lord, let us be ones who bring forth this golden oil together. In Jesus/Yeshua's mighty name. Amen!

CHAPTER 6

Jerusalem: Do You Know Me?

Jesus said, "O Jerusalem, Jerusalem, the one who kills the prophets and stones those who are sent to her! How often I wanted to gather your children together, as a hen gathers her chicks under her wings, but you were not willing! See! Your house is left to you desolate; for I say to you, you shall see Me no more till you say, 'Blessed is He who comes in the name of the Lord!'"

— Matthew 23:37–39

In June 2006, I graduated from my university and completed that portion of my life to the best of my ability. I was a student athlete, a ministry leader, and involved with the community in the Twin Cities: St. Paul and Minneapolis, Minnesota. The student body and faculty nominated me to be the senior class speaker for our commencement ceremony. Again, I was honored to have their reverence and nomination to represent them as the class speaker. After my commencement ceremony, I continued to stay in the Twin Cities area, serving as a youth pastor at a local church.

Due to previous commitments I had made as a youth pastor, I decided to take the Israel trip the following year—in 2007 instead of 2006. The year 2007 proved to be a prophetic swirl of a year that led me across many nations, then back to the United States. After going to Israel and spending time in different regions in that nation and in northern Egypt, I spent a good portion of the summer in Sierra Leone, then finally the United Kingdom.

On July 7, 2007, I got off an airplane from overseas and almost immediately went with some friends into Nashville, Tennessee, to take part in something called "The Call." I did not know what this event truly entailed, but I had committed to go prior to leaving the United States because there was a desire to gather intercessors for fasting and prayer for the nation. How could I not go? The timing was not good for me personally, but I knew in my spirit I was supposed to be there. So I loaded the coach bus that our young adult Bible study group had rented, and we drove down to The Call.

On the way back from Nashville, heading back to the Twin Cities, the Holy Spirit riveted me for days on end. The Holy Spirit dealt with me in a way I had never experienced before or since. I will share a little more about that in chapter 7.

Israel, O Israel! What a journey! I could write a book solely on that 2007 trip alone, but for now I will simply highlight an encounter I had with Jesus in the middle of the night. While I was in Jerusalem, I stayed at a guesthouse in the Old City by Jaffa Gate. I loved the building—and the entire neighborhood, for that matter. As I got to know some of the ladies who were also staying there, I learned more history about the building in which we were staying. A woman named Lydia Prince used to live in the house that we were now using as a Christian guest home. One of the ladies who stayed in the guesthouse with me told me many details during our mealtimes about Lydia Prince and her life's journeys. Her life story deeply impacted me, as I also learned about her husband, Derek Prince. The neighboring building had been converted into a museum and a library to memorialize both of them. I never heard of either of them before, but I knew in my spirit that my staying in their former house had been a divine setup.

After learning more about Lydia Prince, her life, and her journey to Jerusalem, I knew there was a greater purpose to Lydia Prince and me crossing paths by way of her old home. I felt our lives had similar threads and messages. A black woman intercessor from the United States who was living in Israel gave me a book entitled *Appointment in Jerusalem*—and it had been written by Lydia Prince. The Norwegian lady intercessors who were also staying in the guesthouse and the African American woman all prayed over me and told me to read the book because they believed Lydia Prince and I possessed a similar calling. The time I spent at that guest home in Jerusalem was a significant part of my journey to understanding my connection to this beautiful nation.

Traveling across the world does come with its challenges at times. The first leg of my trip had a few major challenges—one of them was my luggage. My luggage had been lost or misplaced on two occasions already, so when I arrived in Israel, I did not have any bags. I had nothing except for my carry-on backpack and the clothes I was wearing. I lived that way for three months! I learned complete dependence on the Lord, especially as a single woman in a foreign land. I'll tell you one thing: He provides! He provided for me every step of the way.

All of that to say, I did not have the best clothes to wear during the trip, so I often wore what was offered to me by others. When I first arrived in Israel in 2007, I unknowingly made my trip during a high holy day season for Jews. I was not aware of this initially, but I did wonder why so many Jews from all over the world were flying into Jerusalem at around the same time. Let's just say the plane ride was a bit wild. Just picture Orthodox Jews from all across the globe, mixed with international tourists and secular Israelis who were traveling to attend parties or outdoor music festivals. The plane ride itself was the stuff movies are made from!

Later, as the flight progressed, I realized it was Shavout: Pentecost was upon us. Many Jews were making preparations to stay up all night long and gather at the Western Wall of the Temple Mount to celebrate the harvest and the giving of the commandments. Of course, I was going to attend the festivities as well! I was not wearing the nicest clothes, but I was not going to let that stop me. I had made up my mind that I was going to be present. I walked the back winding streets of the Old City going into the Temple Mount area some miles away, enjoying every step. There was a childlike excitement and expectation in the air that surrounded me on those back winding streets.

I loved the fact that, depending on what I was wearing, I had the ability to blend into different crowds. Different people from different parts of town each assumed I was one of them. My hair was big and curly, with a few different shades of black, brown, and golden blonde, and I did wear a nose ring at the time in my left nostril. People assumed I was an Ethiopian Jew when I was in Jewish quarters. Muslims assumed I was Muslim while I was in their shuks. Internationals had no idea what I was unless they asked. Most of the street merchants called me a "gypsy." I was grateful that my brown skin and big, curly hair gave me a "pass" to go in and out of wherever I pleased for the most part.

I scaled a high wall that overlooked the entire Temple Mount, then sat there and watched everyone pass by. I saw young Jews gathering and flirting, wearing their best clothes and perfumes. I saw the men, fathers, and rabbis dancing around the city squares. And then I began to weep. There I was, sitting in the very place Jesus had shown me only a year prior. I had never seen buildings and architecture like this before. Yet, there I sat. Then I began to think about Jesus and where He was and what *He* was doing. I remembered how He had sat and gazed at this region of the world from the heavens. I remembered the two of us just sitting there in the clouds, and part of me wondered if He was there again. I missed His Presence.

As I sat and pondered these things, I transitioned from people-watching into praying. I began to pray over every person I saw passing by. "Jesus, as these Jews gather all night long to celebrate Shavout, open their eyes to You, their Messiah! Jesus, let them celebrate You. Lord, let them see You as the fulfillment of the Law and the Prophets. Jesus, I love Your people. Your people will be my people. Their God is my God. And I will follow You wherever You go."

After a few hours of just watching and praying, I realized I needed to move around a bit more. I made my way down to where all the people were, walking around and praying silently to myself. Finally, I made it down to the Western Wall. The rabbis had just finished dancing with Torah in their arms. They were dressed to the max! And the Torah scrolls they held in their arms were completely decked out! I'm talking fabric, colors, silver, and gold, like I've never seen in any other book. *My God, this is beautiful!* I thought.

As I paced the open area in front of the Wall, I caught a glimpse of a bright light. I saw a man from across the corridor. His priestly garments were the most beautiful clothes that I'd ever seen. There were silvers and blues on top of the white threads. The threads seemed to almost glisten. I thought to myself, *My God, who is that?! He must be a very special or important rabbi*. I had seen other rabbis dressed in immaculate garments and robes, but I've never seen clothes like these before! Then the rabbi drew closer, and I saw his face. *My God!* "He is the most beautiful Man I've ever seen! I am going to marry Him." Those words just came out of my mouth like water! I shocked myself by my strong reaction. Then I just stared at Him.

As I began to stare, the Man's eyes went from looking around the crowds to locking in and staring straight into mine. *Whoa. He sees me*, I thought to myself. As He walked closer, I saw that He was, indeed, glowing. All around Him was a small entourage. On every side, He had a small band of men surrounding Him so that no one could touch Him. These men were looking all around but also tending to Him. They moved across the open space like a unit, acting almost like security guards moving an important person through a large crowd.

As I studied the Man more closely, I felt glory begin to fill my body. The closer He came to me, the more I became overwhelmed by the glory. My tongue began to cling to the roof of my mouth. Then just as He was looking at me, He smiled. "Lord, it's You!" It was Jesus! I had never seen Him like that before. There He was, with His disciples, right in the middle of the festivities. Of course, He'd come and take part in Shavout! He is the fulfillment of all prophecy! He is the Law that came down from the mountain of the Lord! The spirit of prophecy is the testimony of Jesus! My God! His hair reached all the way to the ground, and it looked freshly combed and treated. I knew in my heart that He was following the Nazirite vows until His return, including not cutting His hair, which was like brown wool. I wanted to move closer to talk to Him and touch Him, but I was frozen. Only my eyes could move. I couldn't speak or move any other part of my body. The disciples didn't look at me much or acknowledge me any more than anyone else. But Jesus did. *He* knew me. And for as long as I could see Him, His eyes were locked with mine. *He* loved me. And I loved Him. In our exchange, He knew that I knew what He was doing. He also knew that I would've begun to loudly yell and startle others if I were able to speak, so I believe that is why I was placed in a frozen state. He walked right up to me.

As He walked by, I felt His desire for His people. I even saw and felt callings and destinies hanging over various individuals' heads. I knew they just needed to come into fellowship with Him. I saw that one couple was actually secretly close to coming to Jesus, but they feared telling their families for fear of excommunication. I also sensed the deep love He had for so many of them. One person was set apart, away from this, while another was being preserved for that. Jesus was so intentional and so kind regarding His relationships with His people. I felt His pleasure with the disciples, with the crowds—and His pleasure with me. What a humble, perfect, loving, intentional, and sincere Maker He is!

He began walking farther away into the distance, and I was losing sight of Him. I was able to turn my neck and look once more as He looked back and smiled. I knew it was a look to say, *See you later, and I love you.* There is so much more to Jesus and His ways than we could ever know. There is so much more to the natural order of life than we know right now. And there is so much more available to us in the spiritual realms than we realize. As Jesus walked away, my initial thought still rang out: *He is the most beautiful Man I've ever seen!* His Presence then began to diminish, and I was left once again with an ache in my heart. I needed more of Him. I was completely fascinated by His beauty.

My heart's desire became to stay in Israel, and if I had my way, I would relocate full-time to this ancient land. After all, Jesus did call me to Israel. But as I prayed, He told me I needed to go back home to the United States, even though I had no desire to do so. I received so many promises of revival and awakening in Israel, and my feet had finally touched *the land.* Now that I was there, He was telling me I would have to go back to the States? I did not understand His ways.

Takeaway

Jesus/Yeshua is the most fascinating and beautiful Person I have ever encountered. The words from Hebrews 1:9 ring true in my spirit: "You loved righteousness and hated wickedness;

therefore God, your God, has set you above your companions by anointing you with the oil of joy" (NIV). Holiness is beautiful. Holiness brings pure joy.

If we want to encounter Jesus and draw closer to His heart, then we must get to know His firstborn brothers, the Jewish people. Although He has been God Almighty from the beginning, He chose to establish one specific people group into which He came down and entered the human storyline. He established a people, and then He became one of them. All His promises and covenants to Israel still remain true to this day. He is faithful and true to every promise that He makes.

If your love for Jesus does not lead you into a deep love and appreciation for the Hebrew people, then I say your love is biased and amiss. If it is your true desire to marry Him one day (the day of His return to the earth, as a member of His bride, the church), then you must get to know His family. You cannot worship a Jesus/Yeshua that you make up in your own mind. You must get to know Him as He is. If the Jewish people are not deeply embedded in your heart, then how can you appropriately help to prepare the earth for His return?

There is coming a day when the people of the earth will have a representative remnant who loves and worship Him. The Jews must come in, as well. The Jews have a significant role to play in the end-time move of God. The nations of the earth have a significant role to play, as well. There cannot be one without the other.

I encourage you to spend time in prayer and ask the Lord about these things. Ask Him about Israel and His heart for the Jewish people. Jerusalem was significant then, it is significant now, and on into the future, it will continue to be at the very epicenter of the purposes of God.

Prayer of Impartation

Raise your hands, open your spirit, and receive this prayer of impartation.

> *Father, I bless this dear reader with might. Father, I ask that he or she would receive the grace and gift of desire to search You out and step into a deeper love relationship with You, King Jesus. Father, I ask for a supernatural transaction of liquid love from above to melt his or her heart for the Hebrew people. Father, show them Your plan for the nations of the earth and Your desires for the Jewish people. I ask that You open his or her eyes to the miracle of the covenant that Your blood purchased.*
>
> *Father, I ask that a cry would rise up from inside of them—a cry much like the cry of Ruth: "Your people shall be my people, and your God, my God" (Ruth 1:16). Let them commit to standing with the Jewish people in every corner of the earth. I ask that You give to them the gift of intercession, tears, and groaning too deep for words so the nation of Israel can be birthed once again and baptized into her awakening and salvation. I declare these things in the powerful name of Yeshua Ha Meshiach. Amen.*

CHAPTER 7

Called to the House of Prayer

Because zeal for Your house has consumed me...

— Psalm 69:9

D uring those transitional years of 2006 and 2007, the Lord was still working in me and shattering the paradigms of what I believed ministry looked like. I spent a lot of time in this season of life in prayer and fasting. During these times of prayer and waiting on Him, I began to weep over the verse in Psalm 69 that says, "Zeal for Your house has consumed me" (verse 9 HCSB). The New King James Version says, "Zeal for Your house has eaten me up." Deep within my spirit, this verse resonated with the true cry of my heart.

As I waited on the Lord and asked Him for direction and a clear view of my purpose, all I kept hearing were these resounding words: *Build My house. Build My house. Build My house.*

Lord, what does that even mean? I wondered. *What is Your house?* That was my first question. Second was this: *How do I build it?* The questions plagued me. The thundering and recurring commands almost became irritating. As I sat down and quieted my soul to pray, those were consistently the first words I heard: *Build My house!*

At the time, I held a pastoral position at a local church. I wondered if that was what He was talking about. Was His house the local church? I had heard lots of language about the local church being the "house of God." But I knew in my spirit that was not what He meant. Why else would He keep saying it over and over? It was as if He'd keep repeating the command over and over until I understood what He meant.

During the month of June in 2007, I began to long more and more for His Presence. Though I was out ministering in the nations, evangelizing, and doing nonprofit work, I still wanted more of Him. I wanted to be with Him in worship and prayer. For a portion of the summer, my team and I were going door to door in small villages in Sierra Leone, Africa. Our purpose was to gather the people, discover what their natural needs were in order to help meet them, and tell them about Jesus and His goodness. Though these methods were good for some people, I did not want to do these things. I had a strong desire to stay in the place of prayer. I told my team leader what was in my heart to do and asked if it would be okay for me to grab my acoustic guitar, go into the vacant church building in the village, and worship and pray alone. I'd cover the teams who were going door to door in prayer, as well as command doors to open in the Spirit for an in-breaking of His kingdom power.

Sierra Leone had been ravished by a ten-year-long war, and many parts of the nation lay in ruin. Most of the nation at that point was made up of religious Muslims, but others were animists. Less than 2 percent of the entire nation's population were Christians, so I knew much work needed to be done, both in the natural and in the spiritual places. I had lived long enough to know the two were dynamically connected. The spiritual realm directly affects the natural realm, and to shift one, we must first shift the other. I honestly felt in my spirit that the best place for me to be was in a place of worship and prayer.

So, with the permission of my team leader, I grabbed my guitar and off I went to the empty, run-down cement structure that served as a church. I paced, sang, prayed, and played my guitar for some time. At first, the atmosphere seemed a bit rough. My prayers seemed to only go as far as a few feet. It took some time spent in worship and prayer before I began to feel a shift in the room. When I felt the shift, I began to sing high praises to the Lord. Powerful new songs began to flow from my inner being. I felt that pure liquid glory coming from above, entering my body, then flowing out of my mouth.

After a few minutes of flowing in worship and spontaneous praise, a new level of freedom came into the room. Then I began to hear little voices. To my surprise, some local children had heard me singing and worshiping the Lord. This was a rural village with no electricity, so I was surprised someone had heard me all the way out in the vacant areas surrounding the dilapidated church building. I had not seen anyone around the village the entire day, so I was surprised to see the little brown faces peering into the cement building with no doors or windows left. I waved my arm for them to come in, then continued to sing high praises to Jesus and they joined in. One little boy left, then came back with his friends and their tribal drums. They began to drum as I played and sang. These little children were mighty warriors, and as they struck the drums, I felt the earth begin to shake, and a new sound of praise emerged. A beautiful sound filled the atmosphere.

The sound of the drums caused the entire village to come together. The church building began to fill, and it had reached capacity before I even realized that the building was *too* full. The people were beginning to overheat, so we all moved outside, where everyone could hear my voice. They said, "Your voice is so sweet! Please don't stop singing."

Soon I saw our team coming around. They were amazed and said, "No wonder we didn't have much success going door to door—the entire town is here!" I sang a few more songs and then handed them over to the native speakers and the known evangelists on my team. I felt like I had done my part in the team ministry and completed what I needed to do. My role in performing prophetic intercession and worship shifted the atmosphere for the King of Glory to come in. And as He came, the Holy Spirit drew the entire town to Him. What a fruitful day we had in the Lord!

From that point on, I gained a new confidence in my role in the body of Christ. Praying, worshiping, and interceding hadn't been taught much in Bible college, but it was my calling from heaven. I needed to be free from man-made systems and walk in the design of heaven. An entire village was able to hear the Gospel in part because of my decision to follow the Holy Spirit into the place of worship and intercession.

Takeaway

Intercession is a valid calling. So, intercessors in the earth, be encouraged! Your role is one of the most valuable roles in the kingdom. The Lord is intentional when He raises up intercessors, those who will stand in the gap between the present state of being and the fullness of what Jesus' blood purchased. Be released into your God-given assignment. Much like He did with the prophet Ezekiel, the Lord is asking us to partner with Him by opening our mouths and declaring the things He tells us to declare. This, indeed, is divine partnership.

If you are not satisfied with business as usual, then know you are justified in your holy discontentment. Intercessors, through agreement as kingdom ambassadors, shift atmospheres and create the future through their words, prayers, decrees, and declarations. Jesus Himself is the Great Intercessor, who lives to intercede. Even now He makes intercession for us before the Father.

In the days and years to come, the intercession of the people of God will continue as they gather together in groups of two or more and shift regions through prayer, worship, decrees, and declarations. This is the government of God. The ruling and reigning ones are the living stones of God's *ecclesia* (church) who govern the earth from the place of kingdom authority. We are already seated with Christ in heavenly places because of what Jesus' blood purchased for us. Now it is time for us to take our place as the children of God and begin to rule and reign and execute His judgments in the earth.

Prayer of Impartation

Raise your hands and open your spirit man as I bless you.

Father, King of kings, and Lord of lords, Jesus, our Great Intercessor, who ever lives to intercede for us, release travail in Your intercessors on the earth like fireballs from heaven. For those who are called to birth Your purposes through prayer and intercession, Lord, grace them with the gift of travail. Father, brand their spirits with discontent for prayer meetings that don't birth the answers. Lord, release the groanings that are too deep for words.

Holy Spirit, teach Your people to pray. Release their tongues. Let tongues of fire fall now and baptize Your people with the Spirit of burning and holy fire. Let this dear reader transition from being one who prays to becoming a living and breathing house of prayer themselves in their personhood, so that wherever they go, so goes Your Spirit, and the answer to every problem or disparity from Your intended kingdom purposes. Fill them now, in the mighty name of Jesus. Amen.

THE FACELESS MAN— THE SONG OF THE LORD

After spending time in Sierra Leone and Israel, I traveled back home to the United States. As soon as I arrived back in the Twin Cities, Minneapolis–St. Paul, Minnesota, I connected with my friends, with only having a day or two before we were to take a bus down to Nashville, Tennessee, for The Call meeting on July 7, 2007. I was tired from travel and did not feel like being around a lot of people, but I knew I had made the commitment, so I needed to go. I was still adjusting to being back in the States, and I was experiencing a fair amount of culture shock, considering the differences in lifestyles from Africa to Europe to the Middle East, and then back to the United States. Yet I chose to put my culture shock aside and joined my friends on the hours-long bus ride down to the The Call.

Lo and behold, the entire trip was, indeed, ordained by the Lord. The messages coming from the platform were the messages of my heart. Who were these people who carried such a similar thread? I was shocked to hear of the similar storylines and even the same verses of Scripture being referenced. How refreshing! This was a gathering of true intercessors. *Lord, You do have intercessors being raised up in America!* Many significant things happened during this event, but for me, personally, what happened on the road back home is what marked me forever.

My friends and spiritual community members who had rented the coach bus to go down to the event had been fasting for forty days prior to the gathering. And now, everyone was buzzing with Holy Spirit energy on the ride back home. We broke out into prayer and worship several different times on the ride down to Nashville and on the ride back up to Minnesota. But on the return trip to the Twin Cities, the Holy Spirit actually took over and turned that bus into a corridor of glory!

I remember sitting there in my seat as I began to sing out in the Spirit with the song of the Lord. Others began to pray and groan in the Spirit. But as I looked straight ahead, I must've begun to see in the Spirit, because about three rows up and to my left, I watched a man whom I did not know stand up, turn around, and look at me. But the Man was full of power and authority. He was not anyone from our spiritual community who had come down to the gathering with us. And when He stood up and turned around, I saw that He did not have a face. Then, before I could respond, He opened His mouth and forcefully blew His breath on me. Wind, power, and glory came from His breath and went directly into my spirit. I think half the people on the bus all fell over or flew backward.

Then I began to sing out in a way and with a force that I had never had before. I began singing, "Hosanna, hosanna, in the highest." When I sang, my roommate at the time began to sing along with me as she slid back into her chair. At that moment, holy pandemonium broke out in the bus. People began screaming, wailing, and rolling up and down the aisles. Some people crawled under the bus seats looking for a place to get low in the Presence. *My God! What is happening?* I wondered. To this day, I do not know everything that transpired on that bus, but I do know that many of the people there were marked forever.

Later that night when I got home, I lay down to sleep. A friend stayed the night with me because she was too tired to drive back to her home. Instead of staying in my room, we set up the pull-out-bed from inside the couch in my living room. We both spoke for a while, then fell asleep. Sometime in the night when I was dreaming, that same Faceless Man came back into my space. He blew on me again, and I flew into the air. He blew on me again, and I was all the way up into the air. My body was up in the air and very near to the ceiling. I covered my face so it wouldn't smack the ceiling. "Aahh!" I began to scream. *Boom!* I fell back down on the pull-out-bed, wide awake, and I knew again that something holy was happening. I had never flown through the air like that before. There were times when the Holy Spirit had moved in a powerful way and

I was thrown backward a few feet and was then slain in the Spirit. But this was something completely different. I was going up into the air instead of falling to the ground!

One more time He blew with a force from heaven, and up I went, scraping the ceiling—this time with parts of my body and feet—before coming back down onto the bed. This was all about worship. Each time He blew on me was for the release of the song of the Lord through the Holy Spirit. I knew that in the days to come the Holy Spirit would move through me in waves of glory, and as I sang, He would release the atmosphere and resources of heaven.

Much to my surprise, my friend was still sound asleep despite all the commotion! She was the same roommate I had had during my college days, and even then, she slept through some angelic encounters when I was screaming and yelling and power swirled all around. At times I even hit her so that she'd wake up and see what was happening, but she would just snore and stay in a deep sleep. I thought, *Lord, there is no escaping this.* So I endured the riveting encounter and simply talked to the Lord about what this all meant.

Takeaway

In these last days, the Lord is gathering His people unto Himself. We, His people, will walk in unprecedented power, miracles, signs, and wonders. The things Jesus does in and through us will make the book of Acts look like kindergarten. Jesus is ready to release the power referred to in John 14. He promised His people would go forth in the strength of the Lord and the power of His might, and that we would do even greater works than He did when He walked the earth.

Jesus walked on water, healed the sick, raised the dead, delivered the brokenhearted, restored people's souls, taught, preached, and did many other things that were not recorded in Scripture. All these things are the foundation on which we are to stand. The sad reality is, many Christians and people who claim to be followers of Jesus do not even walk in the basic works and manifestation of His Spirit's power. We marvel at a miracle that happens now and then, but the truth is, a supernatural life should be Christianity 101. All believers are supposed to be living lives that display the supernatural power of almighty God.

We must get back to the foundations so we can go forward into greater works. Sing, daughters of Zion. Sing, sons of God! In these last days, the pure glory will transfer to the people at the sound. Anointed words and sounds, utterances through song, spoken words, even rap are going to break forth. Lift up your voice, for a new sound is coming!

Prayer of Impartation

Lift your hands and open your spirit man as I pray this blessing and impartation over you!

> *Father of glory, Lord of the harvest, the One whose throne is above every other throne, Thunder from heaven! Release the new sound upon Your sons and daughters of thunder. Let a cry arise from Your people. May they discover their voice. Let their DNA begin to sing the song of the Lord. I call into activation every spiritual gift, and Lord, I declare that You fan it into flame. Let this dear reader say yes to picking up his or*

her instruments again and using them to glorify the Lamb. I call for new songs and new sounds to come forth. Lord, release songs about the fear of the Lord and the beauty of Jesus. Release frequencies that heal, save, and deliver.

Lord, raise up a new breed of worship leaders, songwriters, singers, rappers, musicians, and multimedia Levites who are jealous for Your glory and zealous for Your house. Lord of the harvest, baptize them with a Spirit of burning and holy fire from Your altar. Purify the sons of Levi, the priests, those who are called to stand before You and minister to You, O great Lord of the whole earth.

THE CALL TO THE INTERNATIONAL HOUSE OF PRAYER— BICKLE ON INTERSTATE 35

One of my dear friends from the volleyball team at my university graduated a year prior to me. She went down to Kansas City, Missouri, to take part in a mission organization, and I supported her and encouraged her in the transition. I did not know anything about the organization, but she mentioned prayer, worship, and intercession, and I knew she could not go wrong being involved in a ministry with that focus.

After spending some time down at the organization, she was so excited. She began to call me regularly and tell me how she knew this place was for me. They used some of the same Scriptures that I used as pillars of my life. She invited me to a conference, but I did not want to attend. I did not like conferences, and I did not like hype, so I just wrote off her enthusiasm as being from someone who was optimistic about the "next best thing" in her life. I just wanted Jesus and His fullness. Between Bible school, traveling for ministry, and pastoring, I had already seen my fair share of hype, and I was over all of that.

My friend knew my stubborn personality, and she said, "Fine, Joma. I will send you some teachings from the ministry. I know you love good teaching! You can listen to them as you drive and such." I accepted her offer, and she began to tell me about certain leaders and their sermon titles. Then she said, "Oh, you'll love this one. It is from Mike Bickle." *Whooaaa, there was that name!* Back in 2005, when I had that encounter in prevailing prayer and I saw the vision of war coming to our land, that was the name Jesus had given me: *Bickle.*

I did not tell her, but my spirit was so shocked that I nearly swerved my car when I was driving on Interstate 35 in Minneapolis. I calmly asked her, "Who is that?"

Her response was, "You don't know who Mike Bickle is?"

"No. Why should I?"

"Well, he's only the director of the International House of Prayer in Kansas City!"

"Oh… well, please, yes, do send me that teaching," I replied.

I knew from that point on, I would have to make a trip to visit her in Kansas City. *O Lord, there is that name… You gave to me back in 2005: "Bickle, you need to be where this person is."* So, I went down to visit her once or twice, before she invited me and a few friends from our college volleyball team to attend a conference called Onething. While I was there, I heard some great teachings and messages, and I sensed the Lord had significant and sincere people gathered in that place. However I had no desire to ever move to Kansas City or be involved in the ministry at IHOPKC. I enjoyed the Twin Cities in Minneapolis, being a youth pastor, and traveling overseas to minister to orphaned children.

I was reluctant and a bit stubborn, but by August 2007, I went off to IHOPKC for a six-month internship training program. Those months proved to be the finishing touches that Jesus used to shatter my current paradigm of ministry. I received from teachers and leaders who not only believed what I believed, but they had decades more experience than me. They had obtained depth in the Word, and they possessed the ability to explain with clarity some things I had been pondering for years.

When they shared their prophetic history, I discovered my life, encounters, and visions were, incredibly, interwoven with theirs. Wow! "Build My house." *Lord, Your house is the House of Prayer! Oh, Lord! Now I see!* Just a few years earlier, I had been considering whether my life in God was off-track due to the disconnect I felt from believers and leaders around me. Those six months allowed me to detox from the last ten years of denominational ministry. The Lord used those six months to put me on a trajectory to build His house—in the United States, in African nations, and also in Israel.

Takeaway

One of the prophetic promises Jesus gave the House of Prayer movement was this: *I am going to change the understanding and expression of Christianity in one generation.* Jesus is changing the understanding and expression of His body in the earth. I believe this is a loaded statement on many levels, and at each point of meaning, we, His people, must respond accordingly.

As the body of Christ, we must begin to function as a House of Prayer once again. In Isaiah 56:7–8, the Lord clearly stated that His house would be called a House of Prayer for all nations. As the church, we must function as a gathering place for prayer. Our Western idea of a church building that is used to house a few meetings a week for teaching, preaching, or worship is not what Jesus desires. He desires gathering places where believers daily come together, pray, fellowship, and worship.

We as the church are not merely a building—we are His living stones. We are the governing body. We are called to govern, rule, and reign over the universe, the multiverse, and the cosmos, being in Christ. We are now one in the Messiah. When Jesus said He would "tear down this temple and raise it up again in three days," He spoke of His body. His body is now the temple, and we are now in Him. As darkness increases in the earth, we must learn to function as ruling and reigning ones, for He has made us as kings and priests. Darkness and the agendas of darkness are not too powerful for our King, Jesus, and therefore they are not too powerful for us. We are to govern and execute His judgments here in the earth realm with our positioning in the heavenly realms.

"Church," as it has been expressed in the past decades in the Western world, is not going to survive what lies just ahead of us. We must mature as His people, and we must become His living, breathing Houses of Prayer. After we manifest our bodies, souls, and spirits as three-part beings and become individual Houses of Prayer, we need to gather together as a corporate body, an *ecclesia* that governs regions together. We are His body, made up of Living Stones.

The House of Prayer is not just meant for worship and prayer, but it is also for executing justice and righteousness in the realms. Part of our identity as mature sons and daughters of God and a mature bride of Christ is to come into the full expression of what Jesus said of His House. The bottom line is that the Lord desires every believer and believing community to become Houses of Prayer. This is a part of the change in the understanding and expression of Christianity in this generation.

Prayer of Impartation

Raise your hands, open your spirit, and receive this blessing.

> *Father, I thank You that Your plans are grand, and they far exceed any expectations or concepts we have in our minds. Father, I thank You that in Your house there are many rooms, because Jesus told us there are places You have prepared for us. Lord in heaven, I ask that zeal for Your house will consume the receiver of this prayer.*
>
> *I pray for an impartation of fire and burning to come and ignite an unquenchable fire in this dear*

reader for Your Presence. As deep calls out unto deep, Lord, let their souls burn with holy dissatisfaction for the world and all its systems. But in its place, let fire come from Your throne and set them apart for Your glory. Lord, Your ministers are flames of fire, so set them on fire! Set them on fire and let them burn here, there, and everywhere You send them. In the matchless name of Jesus. Amen!

CHAPTER 8

Significant Dreams/ Visions for The House of Prayer Movement

You also, son of man, take a clay tablet and lay it before you, and portray on it a city, Jerusalem. Lay siege against it, build a siege wall against it, and heap up a mound against it; set camps against it also, and place battering rams against it all around. Moreover take for yourself an iron plate, and set it as an iron wall between you and the city. Set your face against it, and it shall be besieged, and you shall lay siege against it. This will be a sign to the house of Israel.

— Ezekiel 4:1–3

JESUS RECEIVING HIS PRAISE—IN THE MIDDLE OF THE CITY STREET

After spending those initial six months at the International House of Prayer in Kansas City, much to my surprise, the Lord instructed me to leave my youth pastor position in the Twin Cities, relocate to Kansas City, and join the full-time staff at IHOPKC. During the first few years of being a staff member there, I served the missions base in various capacities, from leading worship and training to helping run summer camps and building a new teen ministry.

During a service one day, I was struggling to enter into worship. The room felt empty and lifeless, and the music that was playing, in my opinion, was so dry that I could barely tolerate it. Don't get me wrong—many of the singers, musicians, and worship leaders at the House of Prayer during that time were anointed and carried a beautiful measure of God's glory. But because IHOPKC is a 24/7 missions base that, at its core, is a continual prayer and worship meeting around the clock, day and night, there are always singers and musicians leading in worship. Some of the worship sets were downright dry. Others were full of fire. There is grace for the journey.

However, this weekend's service seemed extra dry to me, so I sat down and began to meditate on the beauty and goodness of the Lord. I was personally missing the vibrancy, color, sounds, and different expressions of worship that I used to enjoy prior to being immersed full-time at the House of Prayer in Kansas City. So I tuned out the music and began to worship Jesus for the beauty that He was, is, and will forever be.

As I began to practice this level of worship, much to my surprise, I entered an open vision. I was wide awake, yet it was as if a portal had opened before me. I saw in vivid color a scene open right in front of me, and I was drawn away into this new vision. The room in which I was sitting during the worship service disappeared, and I fully stepped into this different reality.

There was so much sound, lights, and color. An intoxicating cadence began to fill my soul. Drummers were drumming rhythms that made me want to move and dance. As I looked, I saw a group of young people coming my way. They appeared to be in their teens and twenties, urban young people. Their dress and the way they moved told me they were from the cities. Most of them were black, some of them were Asian, others were white, and there was a large group of Latinos.

As I continued to watch, the setting grew loud and seemingly tense. I wasn't sure what was going to occur. I began to wonder why all these young people were gathering in the streets. *Is everything going to be okay,* I wondered, *or will there be some type of confrontation?* As I was pondering this, they all began to fall into line. They were marching to the cadence of the drumbeats. They began to stomp and step in line as if they were marching in a militant and powerful fashion. I wondered where they were going. Then the sight and feeling of the scene transformed from a slightly disturbing and troublesome event into a beautiful and colorful sight to behold. I looked and then realized they had begun to fill the street and were marching toward an intersection. As I watched, there were three other groups of young people coming from all four directions of the city street. They were marching in from all directions.

From the north they stomped, from the east they marched, from the west they danced, and from the south they yelled. Something was culminating. Something cataclysmic was about to happen! But what was the gathering point? The longer I watched, the more I realized they were all in unity. Some of them grabbed cans of spray-paint and began to spray-paint on banners. Then others grabbed the banners and began to wave them over each of their regiments. The scene began to intensify. The more they created, the louder their voices became, and the more militantly they marched.

In front of the ones who marched with banners, I saw a number of young Latino men break out of the ranks to lead. They all filed to the front and edges and began to breakdance around those who were marching. They began to dance and spin in every direction, yet they kept moving forward with those marching. As I continued to watch, I saw that from every direction they were going to meet and collide in the middle of the intersection.

With the drum cadence booming, the marchers yelled in unison. Those with the beautiful, spray-painted banners waved them in the air, and the break dancers moved their way to the front of each group. The four groups coming from all different directions converged upon one another, and they met at the intersection. The break dancers then formed a circle in the middle of the city intersection. Then, from every direction—from the north to the south to the east to the west—they all stopped marching. They stood in place and began to rap and chant and scream and dance. *What a powerful sound*, I thought.

Then I looked and saw, to my amazement, what was going on at the very center of the intersection. There stood Jesus.

He was in the middle of the city intersection, He raised His arms in the air, and He received His worship! He closed His eyes, threw His head back, and began to bounce and dance like someone would dance to heavy bass–laden house music. He inhaled the praise like it was a thick fragrance of worship and adoration. The more He received His praise, the louder the young people yelled.

I began to weep. Jesus was receiving His worship and taking delight in the urban expressions of worship and praise. I knew in my heart that this was my people group, as well. I wept over the beauty of King Jesus receiving His worship with rap and spray paint and dance. In that moment He freed my heart to worship Him in different ways. I love bass, rap, spray-paint art, graffiti, and the urban expressions. He showed me there is an entire people group out there, waiting to bring their song and expression to Him, and He takes delight in it. He desires their worship. He enjoys the sounds and sights. He breathes it in like an intoxicating fragrance. I was undone.

After some time, I found myself back in the church building. The portal that had been in front of me disappeared, and I was back in the service, where the same dry songs were being sung, and most people were standing stoically in place. Yet there I sat in my seat, completely undone by the beauty of Jesus and His desire for worship, and not just for the contemporary Christian worship sounds I was listening to. I was left still trying to catch my breath as I processed what I had just seen and experienced. Jesus loves and desires the sounds of house music, rap, Latino and Caribbean music, and all the urban expressions of worship.

Takeaway

An entire generation of young people is coming out of hip-hop and into IHOP (the realities of Intercession, Holiness, Offerings to the Poor, and Power in the Prophetic). The culture— the *religion*—of hip-hop leads only to death. But Jesus came to bring us all life, and He gave His life so we could live ours to the fullest. For those who love the different sounds and expressions that come from rap, house music, stomp, reggaeton, and more, know that Jesus loves those sounds, too! He is waiting to receive His worship from these tribes.

If you are part of this tribe, then lift your voice! Dance your dance! Let the fullness of your expression in Him come out! There is a day coming when the streets are going to be full of this new sound. Heaven will begin to invade the earth again, and it will be at the sights, sounds, and expressions of those who left hip-hop and came into IHOP (not only literal houses of prayer, but those that hold the same core values and standards). They are leaving the false and coming into the real. They will leave Babylon and Babylonian systems and come into the kingdom of the Son.

Prayer of Impartation

Raise your hands. Open your spirit, and receive this blessing.

> *Father, I thank You that in Your throne room there is lightning, thunder, and voices. Your voice causes everyone in Your temple to cry out, "Glory!" Lord, let new songs and rhythms come forth from this generation. Songs, hymns, and spiritual songs, Lord, let*

them come forth! Lord, I speak a release over all the creatives who were told their expressions weren'nt welcome in Christian circles. I declare freedom over their creative hearts! I declare freedom over their souls! And I bless their spirits to create and express unique forms of worship for the living God. Let there be singing in the streets, the hallways, the highways, and the byways. Awaken joy and creativity once again, for You said that not only would You gather us into Your house, but, Lord, You promised to make us joyful there. Lord, restore the joy!

DREAM OF CATCHING BABIES

One day I lay down to take a nap. Little did I know, I was going to have a life-changing dream or encounter that would mark me forever. The dream was very detailed, and to this day, it felt like much more than a dream. It was as if I was actually there. The experience of the encounter was all-consuming.

At the beginning of the dream, I saw a large building. The building was extremely large. I do not know how many floors were in it, but it reached far up into the sky. The building reminded me of one of the skyscrapers in downtown Chicago. The building was massive, like a skyscraper that had many different floors, hotels, companies, and organizations residing inside of it. The lower levels contained nicer sit-down restaurants as well as fast food chains.

I began to engage with some of the servers and restaurant owners on the lower levels. I was taken aback, to the point of disgust by the level of consumption and the lawlessness that abounded with the staff and servers. I saw in the back rooms there was much drunkenness, perversion, and wild living taking place. It was as if both the workers and the consumers had made their bellies their god, and the employees made self-pleasure their goal to attain. Many of the restaurant staff were working just to support their party habits of excessive drinking, illicit drug use, and casual sexual encounters. Many of the owners knew about the employees and consumers and these lifestyles of addiction and perversion, but they were absolutely fine with making money off the spirits of the air. One of the owners said, "It's called 'wine and spirits' for a reason!" Then he began to laugh at his financial gain.

After witnessing the lower levels, I went up to the middle floors to find training programs and institutions of higher learning. Students and others associated with the programs were living on certain floors of this building. The dorm rooms contained bunk beds, and many of the students had been lulled to sleep. Many were living in deep darkness. It seemed like a dark and heavy blanket covered them, and they had fallen into a deep sleep. Some of the floors and programs associated with this training seemed fancy and highly esteemed, but at the end of each day, the students were clearly under a heaviness and fell prey to deep slumber.

I went up higher to find governmental circles meeting around round tables. I found myself sitting next to certain Supreme Court justices. Initially I wondered why I was in this room, but as time progressed, I became aware that many decisions were being made there for selfish and wicked reasons—and many of these decisions would directly harm young children. So when someone at the table asked for my opinion,

I began to speak as a voice of truth and justice on behalf of the children, the orphaned, and the unborn. I spoke with a conviction and a righteous anger that caused some of these evildoers and plotters to sit back in their chairs in shock. It became clear I was there to plead the case of innocent children, both nationally and internationally. Many of these people were malicious and bent on doing evil, and I knew someone needed to stand up and intervene on behalf of righteousness, justice, and loving-kindness in that room.

From there, I was invited higher, to the very top floor. There I saw other types of government leaders sitting at tables in a boardroom type of setup. One certain person stood up to speak, and I discerned from the beginning that he was a flatterer and a deceiver, that he was pure evil. Although he was a handsome, articulate, charming, well-dressed, and well-spoken individual, he was filled with evil. He almost gleamed like an angel of light, but I knew in my spirit that he was an evil man. After he spoke, everyone clapped and applauded him and his endeavors.

Then people lined up to shake his hand. Many people anxiously repositioned themselves just to get closer to him in hopes to have a conversation or receive a handshake, but I just stood back and watched him. I watched as he made his way around the room and then exited the boardroom. I watched him very closely, because I knew he was up to something twisted and evil.

When the vision turned to the nighttime, I went to where I was sleeping, still in the building, and I began to turn back my sheets. But really, I was not tired enough to go to sleep. So I decided to go out and walk the hallways. I walked up and down a few floors of the building, thinking and pondering the day—and then I saw it. The same man whom all the political leaders were adoring was awake, as well. I watched as he took some papers and lit them on fire, then he took those on-fire papers and distributed them through the hallways of the building. He had lit the entire building on fire! Disgust and disdain, mixed with righteous anger and alarm, flooded my being. I yelled and ran after him, but he escaped down a back cement stairway. The last look on his face was one that proclaimed, *They will never even believe you*, as he disappeared out of sight. He had set the entire building on fire! I was furious.

I wanted to chase him down, but there was no time. I ran back to my sleeping quarters and began to yell to awaken the students. "Wake up! Wake up! The building is on fire!" I shouted while knocking frantically on the doors, but no one was listening. No one smelled the smoke or felt the heat, because they had been lulled into a deep sleep. The building was massive and large, and I knew people needed to evacuate, and that if they waited too long, it would be too late. I began to run to many different floors, yelling for people to get to safety, but still no one responded. So, I decided to go outside and yell. Maybe people from the outside would hear and listen and spread the word. The fire was currently only at the top floors, but I knew it would quickly spread, even in a sturdy and intentionally built structure such as this.

I went outside and yelled, "The building is on fire! Get out! He set the building on fire! Get out!" It was as if I was yelling into the air—where was everyone? Only a few ladies responded. They ran over to me, and I told them what happened. One of them said, "Oh no! The children!" "Yes!" I said as I grasped my head in disbelief. I remembered that on the third and fourth floors of the building, there had been many, many children. No one else listened to me, and I knew the ladies and I were the only help available to get them to safety.

We ran to the front of the building, and sure enough we could see there were many children trapped inside. I saw some small fires beginning to spread from the top of the building downward. Our only choice was to have someone go and throw them out of the windows. There were too few of us to run back and forth and get them one at a time. So I stood there on the ground, and the ladies were there to help me organize the kids and keep them calm once they were out to safety.

As I was trying to devise a plan, I looked up at the fourth-floor windows and saw someone waving at me. A female nurse was waving her hand. She was faceless, yet I somehow knew she was there to help—and I knew it was supernatural help. She looked at me and nodded her head. She broke the window and began to throw the kids down. I began to catch them—one by one. I would catch a child and then give the child to one of the ladies for care. I knew we had to move quickly if we were going to get them all to safety. I yelled to the faceless nurse to keep throwing out the children. She was dropping them in baskets with blankets, but soon the baskets ran out. I yelled, "It's okay—keep going! I'll catch them!" I found myself running back and forth like a basketball practice sprinting drill. I ran as quickly as possible from line to line, catching the kids and handing them over to the women. I began to think, *We won't have enough time at this rate to get them all out! Lord, we need more help. We need another strategy!* But I didn't have the luxury to stop running back and forth to find more help.

At that point, I was in a life-or-death situation trying to save each and every child.

After some time, I began to sweat profusely. The kids began to decrease in age. First the four-year-olds came down, then the three-year-olds, then the two-year-olds. I began to worry. If the kids got any younger, they would become more fragile, making them more difficult to catch. Because they would not be as balanced and strong, I worried they might land in my arms wrong and be injured. I was running as fast as I could, but I was not moving fast enough. The nurse just kept throwing them down. And then some of the children began to hit the pavement!

I saw some of their legs break, and I screamed. *My God!* I grabbed them and gave them to the ladies, slightly in shock as I continued on. More children began to hit the ground—one-year-olds and babies. They began to fall to their deaths.

No! I watched as they hit the pavement. Blood splattered everywhere. When I saw another child die as they hit the ground, I somehow supernaturally knew their entire life story. When each child died, I knew their name, their age, their ethnicity, and what they had been called to do on the earth: Isaiah, a twin black boy, Elijah his brother. Tiffany, a biracial girl—black and white. Brooke, a white girl. *Lord!* Overcome with grief and stained by their blood, I kept running between their mangled bodies, still trying to catch as many children as possible.

I began to weep as I ran. Tears and sweat began to blur my vision, and as I attempted to dry my face by wiping it with my shirt, blood was smeared all over my face and shirt. Their precious blood stained the ground, and now it had stained me!

I knew at that point I could not catch them all, and the trauma of it caused me to go into a heartbroken shock. My body continued to move, but my heart and soul were broken within me. Then to my amazement, the children became younger and younger—from nine months old down to six months. Then from six months to three months old. Astonishingly they soon became even younger, until they were still in their womb sacs. I began to catch as many of the squishy, watermelon-sized sacs as I could. These babies were still in the womb! *My God!* At first, they were all different sizes—then they became smaller and smaller, going from watermelon sized to cantaloupe sized. Then smaller: baseball sized and even down to the size of golf balls. The babies were getting younger and younger.

Lord, help! I am catching as many as possible, how can I catch more? This is unjust. Eventually it stopped. The sidewalks were splattered with blood and body parts. I mourned for the children I hadn't been able to catch. But I saw a glimmer of hope when I looked over and saw the ladies taking care of the ones that we *had* been able to save. They had organized them by age group and need, and we made plans to get them to safety.

After the children who remained were safe, I became filled with righteous indignation. Someone was going to pay for this! I ran to the top floor of the building. Filled with fury, I began to search for the evil governmental leader who had caused so much unnecessary death. I was going to require him to tell the truth of what he had caused, and then I was going to pronounce a judgment over his head for his blood guilt.

I stormed into the boardroom on the top floor, and I pointed my finger at the lawless one. I yelled in the company of everyone there, "Tell everyone what you did, or I will decree—"

But before the words finished coming out of my mouth, an explosion went off. Men and women in suits, ties, and business attire had their clothes blown right off them. The power of the explosive blast caused their clothes to be ripped off their bodies. Some were bloodied, while it appeared others were deafened by the blast. Destruction surrounded us. The feeling was one of being stuck in slow motion. The blast left people walking around like they were in a drunken stupor. Blood slowly ran from some of their ears. Most of them could not speak. Papers that had once been important documents were flying in the air, tattered and in pieces.

Takeaway

I believe the building in my dream represents the United States of America. Although we are a beautiful nation, we are full of treachery. We made our bellies and our own desires our god. We feed our souls with sensual and earthly appetites, and we consistently chase comfort. We self-medicate our brokenness with perversion and entertainment, thus distracting us from the severity of the hour in which we are currently living. The statements in Philippians 3:18–19 ring true:

> *For many walk, of whom I have told you often, and now tell you even weeping, that they are the enemies of the cross of Christ: whose end is destruction, whose god is their belly, and whose glory is in their shame—who set their mind on earthly things.*

We as a nation have fallen asleep while we chase our vanities, but the same people whom we praise as our governmental leaders are the same ones who are causing our very collapse. Through deceit, the leaders lead and pull the dark wool over the people's eyes, and all the while the men of lawlessness are actively burning our nation down.

The execution of our babies is our greatest defiling stain. Each child lost was a dream of God's heart that was stolen. The Lord gave us His chosen deliverers, and the enemy is seeking to destroy them. Over sixty million children have been killed in the United States of America since the legalization of abortion in 1973. *But thank You, Jesus, that* Roe v. Wade *was overturned in 2022!* The battle now is being fought in the individual states, and the fighting is fierce to tear down this vile idol. *Lord, let the bloodshed cease. I pray that every state will make abortion illegal. No longer will we offer blood sacrifices to demon entities in our land. Lord, continue to raise up Your deliverers!*

Whenever God gives deliverers to a nation, Satan will seek to destroy them in the womb or before they come to maturity and do great damage to his kingdom. Satan was threatened by Moses and his generation coming forth as deliverers to inherit their land. Satan was threatened in Jesus' generation. In both of those generations, decrees came from governmental places to kill all the children two years old and younger. Moses survived national infanticide. Jesus escaped to Egypt and escaped the infanticide decree in His day. Now Satan is threatened again by the messengers coming at the end of the age. The prophets being slaughtered today are some of Jesus' appointed delivers to our nation and to the nations of the earth. They each have a destiny, and each one is a dream of His heart. Satan is terrified of what these deliverers are about to heap upon his head. But Satan will not stop the plans of Jesus. Though Satan has killed millions, there are many deliverers who escaped this modern-day death decree. And those deliverers will destroy the ranks of darkness and usher in the return of King Jesus.

If our nation does not turn from this treachery, the witness of Jesus in the land will begin to pronounce decrees of judgment to the unrepentant and unrelenting workers of iniquity in the high places of this land.

Prayer of Impartation

Raise your hands, open your spirit, and agree with me in this prayer.

> *Lord, I thank You, King of glory, that You still have great plans for the United States of America. Lord, tear down the veil that blinds the eyes of the people who still sit in darkness. Lord, shine Your light. Let them see clearly and judge rightly. I pray for days of awakening to come. Let revival and restoration sweep across our land. Only the blood of Jesus can atone for our national blood guilt. Thank You for Your spilled-out blood, Jesus, that it still speaks a better word over us than all our sins.*
>
> *Lord, raise up messengers and voices of truth in our nation. Raise up ones like David, Daniel, Shadrach, Meshach, and Abednego. Raise up ones like Phineas and Jael, Deborah, Joseph, and Samson. Lord, give us ones like David's mighty men. Raise up voices, Lord, who will combat the evil schemes of darkness. I shout Your words over them, the same*

decree You gave to Moses: "Let My people go, that they may worship the Lord!"

PRAY FOR EVERY BUILDING THAT MATTERS— JERUSALEM

I have set watchmen on your walls, O Jerusalem;
They shall never hold their peace day or night.
You who make mention of the LORD, do not keep
silent."

— Isaiah 62:6

Years later, in 2018, the Lord was using me to birth another House of Prayer in Clinton, Iowa. I realized at that time that I was launching my seventh House of Prayer. I did not realize at the time, but planting and birthing new praying and worshiping communities that function with an apostolic mantle became my norm. As we were preparing to launch this new House of Prayer in a completely new region and territory, I had another prophetic dream.

As I fell asleep, I was taken up above a certain city. I was aware there was a strong supernatural force with me, and I hovered over the city, then landed on a rooftop. Wow, I was back in Jerusalem! There beside me stood a heavenly messenger. He was clothed in a dark robe, so I did not see his face well, but he spoke with me in English. He showed me different parts of the city, some of the neighborhoods, streets, and then the buildings. The messenger pointed out to me which buildings he especially loved. Then he asked me which buildings were my favorites.

I began to look over the city, and I had a hard time choosing which buildings were my favorites. So I hesitated before I answered. Then he said, "Pick the ones that are your favorites, for all the rest are gong to be destroyed." My heart sank. I knew I couldn't pick my favorite ones because I actually loved all of them. So I responded, "I can't just pick one, or even a few, because I love them all." "Exactly," he said and nodded approvingly. I knew that was the meaning of his questioning. He had pushed me to wrestle with my answer so that I could pray.

From there, the conversation went silent. A sobriety filled my heart for Jerusalem once again. I had been given an assignment from heaven to pray for the city of Jerusalem. I needed to take up the torch again afresh and anew. Not only did I need to step up my prayer covering for Jerusalem, but I needed to use my position in leadership to teach this upcoming generation to pray for her until her salvation comes forth as a lamp that burns.

Takeaway

In Isaiah 62:6, the Lord tells us He has set watchmen on the walls of Jerusalem, to not hold their peace day or night, until He establishes it as a praise in all the earth.

As a House of Prayer and Beauty of Jesus people, we must have His heart for Israel, and we must labor in the place of prayer and various types of intercession for the purposes of the Lord in Jerusalem. There are some in the body of Christ who do not see or know the importance of Israel in these end days.

The Lord and His heart for Israel has not changed. The Lord keeps His covenants and always fulfills His promises. If the Lord does not keep His promises toward Israel, then how and why would we ever expect Him to keep His promises toward us?

We are to lean into the prayers of Romans 11. We must pray for the salvation of Israel, that she would become a lamp that burns. The truth is, Jesus is a Jewish Man, and when He returns, He will set up His throne in Jerusalem. Jerusalem will be called the City of the Great King. It will also be called *Yahweh Shammah*, or "The Lord Is There," as Ezekiel prophesied in his glorious and powerful book of the Bible. The return of Messiah Jesus to the earth will begin His millennial kingdom reign here on the earth. What a glorious time that will be! One thousand years of Jesus reigning, and some of us, His people, will reign with Him and transition the earth, preparing it for the Father of glory to come and dwell again. What a glorious day that will be!

Throughout history, the agents of darkness have been trying to destroy the nation of Israel and prevent the Hebrew people from being in their land. The enemy does not want all the prophecies to be fulfilled. He is trying to prevent the return of the Messiah and his own eternal torment by attempting to extinguish our older brother, Israel.

We as the nations of the earth are to provoke the Jewish people to jealousy as we love, worship, and manifest the glory of Yahweh (their God) in the earth. Yeshua/Jesus is their Messiah and King. Yeshua/Jesus has been Yahweh from the beginning, then He became wrapped in human skin. Yeshua is the God-Man. And we need to make a declaration, much like

Ruth did, "Your people shall be my people, and your God, my God" (Ruth 1:16). We need to be friends of Israel, intercessors for their salvation and fullness. Together as Jewish believers in Messiah and Gentile believers in Messiah, we are to bring forth the golden oil and display His glory in the earth (Zechariah 4:11–14).

Prayer of Impartation

Lord, raise up friends of Zion. Raise up believers who will be voices to and for Your people, Israel. I speak to their eyes to be opened to the significance and importance of the nation of Israel. I speak to their hearts: Be softened. May you feel what Yeshua feels for His people. Lord, I speak forth a Spirit of wisdom and revelation in the knowledge of who You are to come and consume them. I pray that this dear reader will have the opportunity to go spend time in the present-day land of Israel and to contend for its fullness and greatness.

CHAPTER 9

"I Am Coming"

Behold, He is coming with clouds, and every eye will see Him, even they who pierced Him. And all the tribes of the earth will mourn because of Him. Even so, Amen. "I am the Alpha and the Omega, the Beginning and the End," says the Lord, "who is and who was and who is to come, the Almighty."

— Revelation 1:7–8

"I AM COMING IN YOUR LIFETIME"

After my initial heavenly encounter at the age of thirteen, I began to live a life of prayer and fasting. I began to experience the goodness, glory, and power of God as I spent time with Him in elongated seasons of fasting and prayer. I knew I felt closest to Him and most powerful when I was in that state of connectedness. I joined friends and leaders, and I prayed before and after church services as well as in my personal life alone into the late hours of the night. One evening before youth group began on a Wednesday night, I felt the strong presence of the Lord swirling around me. The time came for the service to begin, but I knew the Lord wanted more time alone with me. So after the service, I went into a back room to just linger in His presence.

There, the Lord began to dance with me in that back room. He walked right into that room and enjoyed me. Then, after some time of intimacy, He whispered to my spirit and told me He was coming back in my lifetime, and I needed to be in or out. He needed me to be all-in or all-out. He had a great work for me to do, but I needed to have no mixture in me. I knew His loving-kindness was drawing me and compelling me to walk out the *yes* in my heart. Apparently in my heart and life-style, there was still a measure of mixture with the world, but the Lord wanted me to be fully with Him.

There were still things in my life I needed to let go of so that Jesus would have His full reward in and through me. I could no longer hold on to control of my future. I knew I need-ed to prepare myself for His return, and I felt sobered by the reality that most people are living like He is not coming back. I knew I needed to prepare myself for His return, but I did not have any paradigms or leaders around me at the time who were focusing on the necessity of preparing ourselves for His return. I knew He was going to lead me into new realms of truth and reveal great and mighty things to me. But was I willing to ac-cept the call? With His words ringing in my spirit, I began to have the conviction to count the cost and live like His words are truth.

Takeaway

I believe Jesus' words to be true. Even if I am an older grand-mother by the time He returns, I still believe He is coming. So it is my job to first prepare myself to be His true and faithful witness, and then I need to be a voice to the generations coming behind me that He is, indeed, coming. We need to live in the glorious tension of this reality.

We are not preparing for business as usual. We are not living for a retirement plan. Those days are long gone. The American dream is not the dream of our King Jesus. We are going to endure the most trying time in human history—here and now, in our lifetimes. We must prepare ourselves not only to endure during these times, but to lead in strength, power, and glory during days that Jesus Himself referred to as the Days of Noah: "And just as it was in the days of Noah, so it will be in the time of [the second coming of] the Son of Man" (Like 17:26 AMP). This statement alone holds so much meaning that I will need to discuss it more in depth at a later time.

I will explain in depth at a future time about the days of Noah, the Day of the Lord, the second coming of Jesus, the ruling and reigning witnesses, and the transition of the earth to the next age. We have many things to discuss, but for now, know that King Jesus is coming. He will be here sooner than most of us think, so we must prepare like our lives depend on it—because our lives and the lives of our children and their children *do* depend on it.

Prayer of Impartation

Father, I thank You that all our days are written in Your book. You know the days that You've appointed for us to live. By virtue that the reader of this prayer is alive today, we know You made him or her for such a time as this. They were made for the end-time plan of

*redeeming the earth and ushering in the return of the
King.*

*Lord, I bless them with spiritual hunger and
thirst. I bless them with eye salve so that they would
see. I bless them with the gift of urgency. Lord, let
them live with a conviction of the urgency of the hour
in which we live. Beautiful Messiah Jesus, reveal to
them Your plan and Your wisdom for transitioning the
earth for Your glory.*

*Abba, as the nations rage and the people plot in
vain, raise up voices of truth. Raise up lovers of justice
and equity. Bless them with zeal for Your house and
for the people of Zion. Give them greater understanding about the role of Israel, the globalist and dark
agendas of anti-Christ, and their position during this
epic season of Your story. Give them grace to say yes to
You, no matter the cost of that answer. And give them
joy and grace to endure to the end.*

"YOU ARE GREATLY MISTAKEN!"

About ten years later, I left the House of Prayer in Kansas
City, Missouri, and moved back to St. Paul, Minnesota, to
work in Minneapolis once again. For decades I had been faithful to run with diligence and consistency the race the Lord
had marked out for me. Now, in my early twenties, I began to
get a little fatigued. I saw how other young people were living
around me, and I wanted to ease up on my intensity a bit. I
did not want to go out and intentionally sin or be wild—I just
wanted to relax a bit in my pursuit of Him. I wanted to take a

year off and just hang out. I wanted to go places for recreation and entertainment and actually have a social life. I did not want to be fully given over to all these spiritual battles or to keep myself in hot pursuit of Him. I wondered how so many people seemed to just prosper and live a carefree life. So many young adults around me seemed to be okay in their half-heartedness. I didn't want the dullness that many of them had in their hearts, but I did want to relax a bit and feed my carefree desires for a season.

One day I began to clean my house and ponder these things more deeply. I wanted a break from life. I wanted to serve my flesh for a while. Why did I have to be so serious and focused all the time? One of my friends with whom I had attended Bible school had told me a few days before, "While we were out dating around and partying, you were holding all-night prayer meetings and burying your face in the prayer closet. That's why whenever someone needs real prayer and a breakthrough in their lives, they come to you." I knew she was encouraging me, and at that time I didn't know the goodness and the love of God like I do now, but for some reason I was irritated by her comments. I walked away from our time together feeling justified in my desire to take some time on a spiritual vacation. I took it as an opportunity to back off from the flames of holy consecration that, for some reason, were seared in my heart.

My spirit was not at peace with this desire to take a year off spiritually and go on a "vacation" of sorts, but I knew it was a real inner struggle. I was at limbo within. I began to wash my dishes and clean up the house, then I went into my roommate's room and cleaned up her area a bit as well. I picked up a half-eaten bowl of Fruit Loops with the milk still in it. As I stood up, I heard the Holy Spirit say to me, *How much time do you think you have before Jesus returns?*

Full of a measure of pride, I thought, *Well, I do have a strong prophetic gift, and I know You are coming in my lifetime, but I think I have a long time. I think maybe it will happen when I'm in my fifties or sixties. I still have plenty of time to prepare.*

But before I could open my mouth and give my answer, He already knew my thoughts. A gust of wind came into the room with a force so strong that the bowl of cereal flew out of my hand. Then a voice roared from heaven, "You are greatly mistaken!"

The fear of the Lord filled my home, and I made an altar right there. I got down low in the Presence and just laid there. I had thought I knew something. I had thought I had plenty of time to prepare, but I was full of pride. And I was wrong. That day, afresh and anew, I set myself apart for the Lord.

Someone—me—needed to stay focused and stay faithful, not only for the sake of my own heart and life, but for the sake of the generation coming up behind me. If they are to lead during this dispensation of grace, then someone has to prepare them. *Lord, help me get out of the way.*

Takeaway

The Lord is returning sooner than we all think. The Bible does not tell us the day or the hour of His return, but He does command us to stay sober and vigilant and to know the times and the seasons of His appearing. Only those who are asleep will miss His Second Coming. Only those who are in the dark will miss the day of His appearing. So I warn you to be a people of the light. May your entire body be filled with light!

Jesus will only come as a thief in the night to those who are not prepared. The rest of us are commanded to know the times and the seasons. Prepare yourself! Prepare yourself not only to survive times of great shaking and tribulation, but prepare yourself and the realms of influence that He's given you to shine and lead during these times.

What does it mean to be a witness of Jesus? What does it mean to grow in wisdom and stature? What does it mean that Moses and Aaron, the Old Testament prophets, Elijah, John the Baptist, the early disciples and apostles, and even Jesus Himself were all humans? What Jesus is about to release on His people, the ruling and reigning ones will outshine all of them in gloriously powerful acts and demonstrations of His Spirit's power. In John 14, Jesus says that we will do even greater works than He did (see verse 12). It is time, my friend. It is time to grow, shine, and rise to the calling.

Prayer of Impartation

Father of Glory, You brought the reader of this prayer into the earth realm for such a time as this. Lord, teach him or her Your ways. Reveal to him or her the hope of Your calling. Reveal to him or her what it means to be "in You." May they become bright and shining torches for You and Your purposes in the earth. May they consider serving You an honor and not a burden. Let the fires of holy love burn hotter and consume their desire for worldly comfort, pleasure, and entertainment.

"TELL THEM I AM COMING"

During the chaos of 2020, I spent many times in prayer and fasting. In the middle of all the commotion and chaos that was unfolding in the streets of America during that year, I lay down one night to sleep. But instead of falling asleep, I was caught up in heavenly visions. I was taken back to the New Jerusalem, which is above us in the heavenlies. Some time had passed since my last visit, but this time it was different. The urgency of the visit gripped me. There were no polite pleasantries being spoken. No one was gently speaking to me and briefing me on the appointment with Jesus. I knew the only reason I was there was because I had been summoned.

Before long, I landed right there in a throne room. But this place in the throne room was like a heavenly headquarters. This wasn't the bosom of the Father that I had anticipated. This was an executive briefing room. Jesus stood up as the Leader of the heavenly armies. His seat looked like a throne to me, but it was not like the one in the main throne room, where the Father dwelled.

Jesus had a righteous anger and a zeal in His eyes. He wore a special crown and a robe that looked almost like a glorious cape. He stood up from the throne and looked directly at me. He looked into my face with a gaze I'd never seen before, and He spoke one sentence: "Tell them I AM coming!" Then He walked past me with a flash as His robe created a gust of wind and power that rippled behind Him. My body went backward with the force of His words. I did not even have the time to say anything in response. I was already staring at the back of His head. I just thought, *Well, yes, Sir.* I had never seen Jesus like this before. The power and authority of His voice and countenance caused me to tremble, but in an honoring way.

As I stood there, I realized the other beings that were also in the room were looking at me. The other creatures looked at me as if to ask, *Why are you still standing there? The King told you what to do.*

I thought, *Oh yeah, you all are right. I am a human, okay? Give me some time to gather myself.* But they were right. I had been given a message to release in the earth.

Then, in the blink of an eye, I was back in my bedroom. The fear of the Lord filled my room. *My God!* I prayed. *I have never seen You like this before!* We have entered into a new era now. Heaven is preparing for the return of the King. Here on the earth, we need to be preparing for His return, as well.

Takeaway

I am here to tell you, friend. He is coming! His beauty is astounding, but I can promise you this for sure: You do not want to be caught on the wrong side of King Jesus. You are either in or you are out. You are either for Jesus, or you are against Jesus. The church in the Western world has not done its job to accurately portray who Jesus is to this generation. So I will tell you this: Jesus is coming. Jesus is the King of the universe. Jesus is the King of the multi-verse. And He is coming again. But this time when He comes, it will not be as a Lamb led to the slaughter. His coming will be like the setting from the book of Revelation, chapter 6:

> *I watched as he opened the sixth seal. There was a great earthquake. The sun turned black like sackcloth*

made of goat hair, the whole moon turned blood red,
and the stars in the sky fell to earth, as figs drop from
a fig tree when shaken by a strong wind. The heavens
receded like a scroll being rolled up, and every moun-
tain and island was removed from its place.

Then the kings of the earth, the princes, the gen-
erals, the rich, the mighty, and everyone else, both
slave and free, hid in caves and among the rocks of the
mountains. They called to the mountains and the rocks,
"Fall on us and hide us from the face of him who sits
on the throne and from the wrath of the Lamb! For
the great day of their wrath has come, and who can
withstand it?"

— Revelation 6:12–17 NKJV

When King Jesus comes to the earth this time, He is coming as a Man of War. He is coming as the Conquering King. He is likened to a lion in the Bible. The Lion of the tribe of Judah is the King. In the end, nothing will oppose or challenge His rule. Do not be deceived. Do not confuse His gentleness and mercy with His wrath and power. Do not confuse His humility with His strength. Do not confuse His grace as an acceptance of your unholy lifestyle.

Know that a day is coming soon when you must give an account for your life. Each and every one of us will stand before the throne of God and give an account for our lives. Each of us will stand alone before the Judge of the whole earth. Our friends, parents, spouses, children, mentors, teachers, coaches, and idols will not stand to defend us before His goodness and glory. We will all be laid bare before Him. There is no deceit or guile in Him. There is no manipulating or deceiving Him. So choose wisely. Choose this day whom you will serve.

PSALM 2

Why do the nations rage,
  And the people plot a vain thing?
The kings of the earth set themselves,
  And the rulers take counsel together,
    Against the Lord and against His Anointed,
      saying,
"Let us break Their bonds in pieces
  And cast away Their cords from us."

He who sits in the heavens shall laugh;
  The Lord shall hold them in derision.
Then He shall speak to them in His wrath,
  And distress them in His deep displeasure:
"Yet I have set My King
  On My holy hill of Zion."

"I will declare the decree:
  The Lord has said to Me,
  'You are My Son,
  Today I have begotten You.
Ask of Me, and I will give You
  The nations for Your inheritance,
    And the ends of the earth for Your possession.
You shall break them with a rod of iron;
  You shall dash them to pieces like a potter's vessel.'"

Now therefore, be wise, O kings;
  Be instructed, you judges of the earth.
Serve the Lord with fear,
  And rejoice with trembling.
Kiss the Son, lest He be angry,
  And you perish in the way,
  When His wrath is kindled but a little.
  Blessed are all those who put their trust in Him.

— Verses 1–12 NKJV

As for me, I will spend my days in His house and hastening the day of His return. If the time comes that I pass from this earth realm due to my witness for Jesus, or should my blood be poured out for the sake of His name, may it produce a harvest in the nation in which it was spilt. And you, reader, go forth and make His praise glorious! Let your life be a memorial and a fragrant, burning offering to the most beautiful Man alive—King Jesus.

Grace and peace to you from Him who is and who was and who is to come, and from the seven Spirits who are before His throne, and from Jesus Christ, the faithful witness, the firstborn from the dead, and the ruler over the kings of the earth. To Him who loved us and washed us from our sins in His own blood, and has made us kings and priests to his God and Father, to Him be glory and dominion forever and ever. Amen. Behold, He is coming with the clouds, and every eye will see Him, and even they who pierced Him. And

all the tribes of the earth will mourn because of Him.
Even so, amen.

— Revelation 1:4–7

It is my intention that even in death, my body will be a memorial to the Lord. The tattoos on my left and right arms declare the entirety of my life's message:

In Hebrew Script:

וְשֵׁם־הָעִיר מִיּוֹם יְהֹוָה ׀ שָׁמָּה׃

The name of the city [Jerusalem] from that day on will be: THE LORD IS THERE.

— Ezekiel 48:35 NIV

יְהֹוָה ׀ יִמְלֹךְ לְעֹלָם וָעֶד׃

The Lord reigns for ever and ever!

— Exodus 15:18

Final Takeaway

The call of this book is one of radical devotion. But radical devotion only comes after a radical encounter. It is my desire that my simple *yes* over the years encourages you to run full-strength into the beauty of Jesus. It is my prayer that you have your own encounters with His glory.

I believe that part of our birthright as children of the living God is to see Him. The Bible says that "blessed [and happy] are the pure in heart, for they shall see God" (Matthew 5:8). The eternal Father is our Father. Jesus is our heavenly Bridegroom and King. And the Holy Spirit is our closest Friend. When these Persons are our closest relationships, how can we not see God? Seeing and encountering Jesus is not only for "some people" or those "special prophets and seers." It is for everyone who loves Him.

I firmly believe that one encounter with the Man, Christ Jesus, will change your life forever. From that point on, loving Him becomes easy. Loving Jesus consumes your entire being because you have actually looked upon the One who is love. The fire of His Presence leaps onto you and into you, causing you to begin to burn from within. From that point, nothing will ever satisfy you but His Presence.

The things of the world that once led and guided your desires and plans will be consumed in the fires of holy love. I believe an encounter with Jesus is a necessary step to becoming a true disciple. The confession of those around us should be, "They have been with Jesus." We should smell different, act different, and manifest His glory as image-bearers of Christ wherever we go.

Final Prayer of Impartation

Glorious Jesus, I bless the reader of this prayer with heavenly encounters. Lord, tear the veil from their eyes that they may see. Lord, let them see the King in all His glory. Let them see the Son of Man high and lifted up. Like Jesus when He showed Himself to Peter and John on the Mount of Transfiguration, let them encounter the glory that belonged to You, Jesus, long before You created the worlds.

I call into activation the spirit man of this dear reader, and I bless them with the Spirit of burning and fire. May the holy fire from the heavenly altar consume them. May the eyes of Jesus fall upon them, and may they never be the same again.

Run your race! Run your race! Run to the most beautiful Man I've ever seen. He is good. He is Wisdom. And He only does good things. May you learn to rest and trust in His faithfulness and loving-kindness toward you. He made you and designed you with great intention and purpose, and He commanded your spirit to come into this earth realm for this most fascinating time in His-story. So, I bless you, dear one. I bless you with fullness, righteousness, and perfect peace.

ABOUT THE AUTHOR

Joma Short is a worship leader, singer, musician, rapper, traveling minister, podcast creator, teacher, and public speaker. Her ministry over the past twenty-six years has led her to over ten nations and many other territories. When she is not traveling for ministry, she resides in Kansas City, Missouri, with her two daughters. To further engage with her ministry, visit her website: www.thebeautyofjesus.com.

Milton Keynes UK
Ingram Content Group UK Ltd.
UKHW020728081123
432193UK00018B/697